THE ESSENTIAL WORKBOOK FOR
COMPETITION
MATH
FUNDAMENTALS

WORKBOOK EDITION

유하림(Harim Yoo) 지음

Preface

To. 학부모님과 학생들께

독자 여러분, 반갑습니다. <The Essential Workbook for Competition Math (Fundamentals)>를 구매해주셔서 감사합니다. AMC 10 / 12와 같은 미국 수학 경시대회에서 가장 빠르고 효율적으로 고득점을 내기 위해, 공부해야 하는 문제들이 무엇일까 고민을 많이 했습니다. 이러한 고민 끝에 The Essential Guide to Competition Math (Fundamentals)를 출판하게 되었는데, AMC 10/12 시험에 입문하기 위해 학생들이 알아야 할 것들을 정리하였고, 시험 준비에 초점을 맞춘 교재로 평가합니다.

The Essential Guide to Competition Math (Fundamentals)을 출판한 후, 학생들에게서 받은 Feedback은 문제 수를 조금 더 늘려달라는 요청이 있었고, 이에 맞추어 문제 풀이 교재를 낼 필요성을 느꼈습니다. 이번 교재는 Essential Guide의 문제 풀이라고 볼 수 있고, 현장강의에서는 부교재로 활용했을 때, 효과가 있었습니다. 특히, 개념 편에 해당하는 입문서를 통해 학생들을 지도하면서, 이 워크북 문제를 풀었을 때, 학생들의 실력이 느는 것을 확인할 수 있었습니다.

이 교재는 제 제자들 중 특별히 수학에 재능을 가진 학생들이 많은 피드백을 주었으며, USAMO Qualify를 여러 차례 해왔던 학생이 특별히 관심을 가지고, 세밀한 피드백을 주었습니다. 극상위권이 어떠한 방식으로 생각하는지 눈여겨볼 수 있는 워크북 교재입니다. 많은 관심 부탁 바라며, AMC 10 / 12 시험에서 좋은 성적 거두길 기대합니다.

유하림

About the Author

Harim Yoo

Northwestern University
B.A. in Mathematics and Economics
Founder of Xplosive Math Meet

Prepbooks the author has published in South Korea

The Essential Guide to Prealgebra
The Essential Guide to Algebra 1
The Essential Guide to Geometry
The Essential Guide to Algebra 2
The Essential Guide to Precalculus
The Essential Workbook for SAT Math Level 2
The Essential Guide to SAT Math Level 2
The Essential Guide to IGCSE : Addmath
The Essential Guide to Competition Math (Fundamentals)
The Essential Guide to Number Theory (Competition Math)
The Essential Guide to Counting and Probability (Competition Math)
The Essential Workbook for Geometry
The Essential Workbook for Algebra 2
Brain Teaser 100 : Competition Math Workbook (Volume 1)
Think Through Geometry

Recommendation

이 교재를 적극적으로 활용하기 위해, 저자가 소개하는 교재 활용법입니다.

첫째, 1시간 정도 Problem Set 한 개를 풀 생각을 하고, 문제 풀이를 시작합니다. 기본기에 해당하는 부분이 이미 머릿속에 있다고 가정한 후 교재를 작성하였으므로, 기본기가 부족하다면, The Essential Guide to Competition Math (Fundamentals) 개념 편을 구매하여, 마스터프렙 인터넷 강의 혹은 저자의 현장강의 수업을 수강하도록 합니다.

둘째, 자신의 풀이와 Solution Manual에 있는 풀이를 비교하며, 여러 방식을 유연하게 사고하는 방식에 대해서 고민하고, 공부합니다. 한가지 풀이에만 집중할 것이 아니라, 최대한 사고를 유연하게 하여, 이렇게도 풀어보고 저렇게도 풀어보는 훈련을 합니다.

셋째, 자신이 생각하는 지점이 어느 부분에서 막히는지, 취약한 부분이 어디인지 확인하도록 합니다. 사람마다 취약하게 생각하는 부분이 있습니다. 어떠한 학생은 경우의 수 문제를 힘들어한다거나, 다른 학생은 기하 문제를 어려워합니다. 해당 부분들을 잘 기억해 두었다가, 연습의 양을 늘려야 할 때, 취약한 부분을 보강하는 형식으로 공부합니다.

넷째, 이 교재는 경우의 수와 확률 부분이 강조된 교재입니다. Number Theory와 같은 부분에 대한 문제 풀이가 필요한 학생은 The Essential Guide to Competition Math (Number Theory) 교재를 구매하여, 학습하도록 합니다.

복습하다 보면, 생소하다고 생각한 기법들이 어느샌가 자신의 것이 되었다는 점을 인지하는 시기가 반드시 옵니다. 저도 여러분들을 가르치기 위해, 이러한 문제들을 계속 풀다 보니, 어느 순간 실력이 올라가는 경험한 기억이 납니다. 쉽사리 포기하지 말고, 끝까지 밀어붙이는 훈련 하세요. 반드시 실력이 올라갑니다. 이 말을 굳게 믿고, 도전하세요.

Contents

 # List of Math Competitions

Here's a list of some AMC 10/12 or equivalent exams.

1. AMC 10/12A
2. AMC 10/12B
3. AIME (American Invitational Mathematics Examination)
4. USAMO (USA Mathematical Olympiad)
5. HMMT (Harvard-MIT Mathematics Tournament)
6. PUMaC (Princeton University Mathematics Competition)
7. ARML (American Regions Mathematics League)
8. Purple Comet! Math Meet
9. Mandelbrot Competition
10. MathCounts
11. CEMC Exams

Remember to mention that these exams serve as valuable opportunities to test your skills, challenge yourself, and gain valuable experience in math competitions. Participating in these exams will not only help you gauge your progress but also provide exposure to a variety of problem types and competition formats.

Good luck on your math competition journey!

Designed and Tailored for
Your Successful Journey on Competition Math

" Success is not final, failure is not fatal. "

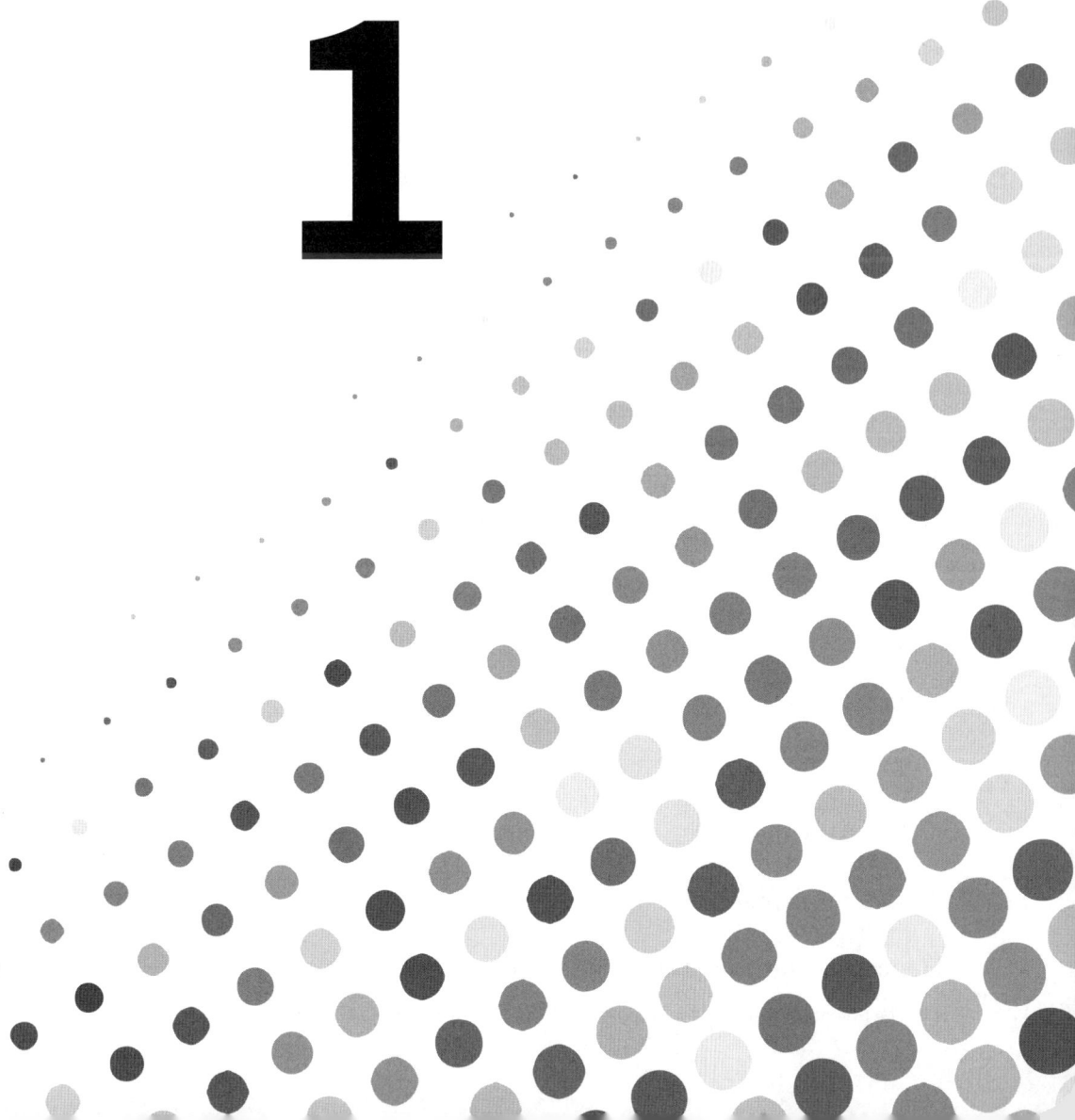

1

Worked-Example #1

If the 16th prime number is 53, what is the 22nd prime number?

(A) 71   (B) 73   (C) 79   (D) 89   (E) 97

The correct answer is (C).

Here is one suggested solution to this problem. First, we should understand that other than 2(the smallest even prime), 3(the smallest odd prime), all other primes can be written as $6k - 1$ or $6k + 1$ for some integer value of k. You can check this by yourself. 5 and 7 are primes; 11 and 13 are primes. These pairs are nice prime pairs, but sometimes not all two become prime pairs. For instance, think about 23 and 25. One can check 23 is a prime number, but 25 is not.

How do we know that $6k \pm 1$ for some integer k is always a prime? This may easily be seen by investigating other number forms.

- $6k + 2 = 2(3k + 1)$: the right-hand side of the equation shows that $6k + 2$ is a multiple of 2. Other than $k = 0$, the given number form must always be even. Since 2 is the only even prime number, we know that other even numbers will not be prime.

- $6k + 3 = 3(2k + 1)$: the right-hand side of the equation shows that $6k + 3$ is a multiple of 3. Other than $k = 0$, the given number must be 3 times odd numbers other than 1. This indicates that $6k + 3$ must be composite, not prime.

- $6k + 4 = 2(3k + 2)$: the right-hand side of the equation shows that $6k + 4$ is a multiple of 2. Just like the first case, this should not be included in the set of primes.

That being written, since the 16th prime is known to be 53, we know it is right next to 54. Using the tool laid out above, we can check that 17th prime is 59, and 18th prime is 61. The following list captures the primes in columns.

1. 16th prime : 53

2. 17th prime : 59

3. $\vdots$

4. 21st prime : 73

5. 22nd prime : 79

Hence, we conclude that 22nd prime number is 79.

Worked-Example #2

> When expressed as a repeating decimal, the fraction $\frac{1}{7}$ is written as $0.142857142857\cdots$ (The 6 digits 142857 continue to repeat.) The digit in the third position to the right of the decimal point is 2. In which one of the following positions to the right of the decimal point will there also be a 2?
>
> (A) 119th   (B) 121st   (C) 123rd   (D) 125th   (E) 126th

The correct answer is (C). Here is one suggested solution to this problem.

Normally, real numbers can be written as three types of decimal numbers.

- Terminating decimals : a decimal number that terminates is exactly equal to a fraction (or rational number). It means that at one point, the decimal expression stops.

- Infinite decimals with repetends : a decimal number that does not terminate yet showing repeating repetends can also be written as a fraction. The only difference between the terminating decimals and infinite decimals with repetends is that the denominator of the reduced fraction may contain primes other than 2 or 5. For instance, $\frac{1}{4} = 0.25$, but $\frac{1}{6} = 0.16666\cdots = 0.1\overline{6}$.

- Infinite decimals with no repetends : a decimal number that cannot be expressed as terminating decimals nor infinite decimals with repetends is known as irrational number. There are algebraic irrational and transcendental irrational numbers. The first type can easily be expressed as radical numbers such as $\sqrt{2}$. On the other hand, the second type can be expressed as π or e.

1. $119 = 6(19) + 5$: this implies that 119th digit after the decimal point must be 5th position in the 20th bundle. This indicates that 119th digit is 5.

2. $121 = 6(20) + 1$: this implies that 121st digit after the decimal point must be 1st position in the 21st bundle. This indicates that 121st digit is 1.

3. $123 = 6(20) + 3$: this implies that 123rd digit after the decimal point must be 3rd position in the 21st bundle. This indicates that 123rd digit is 2.

4. $125 = 6(20) + 5$: this implies that 125th digit after the decimal point must be 5th position in the 21st bundle. This indicates that 125th digit is 5.

5. $126 = 6(21)$: this implies that 126th digit after the decimal point must be 6th position in the 21st bundle. This indicates that 126th digit is 7.

According to each calculation, we conclude that a 123rd digit is 2.

Worked-Example #3

There are three times as many boys as girls in a room. If four boys and four girls leave the room, then there will be five times as many boys as girls in the room. In total, how many boys and girls were in the room originally?

(A) 16   (B) 20   (C) 24   (D) 32   (E) 40

The correct answer is (D).

Here is one suggested solution to this problem. First, we have to set up equations or expressions to solve the given problems. We label the variables in order to set up equations. In this case, boys and girls are unknowns, so we have 2 variables. This suggests that we must set up 2 equations.

If you see a phrase about three times as A as B is, then we can generally write down as $A = 3B$. Paraphrasing sentences into math equation is important in algebra problems. Let b be the original number of boys and g the number of girls in the room. Then,

$$\begin{cases} b = 3g \\ (b - 4) = 5(g - 4) \end{cases}$$

In order to solve for b and g, we either eliminate or substitute one variable. Since $b = 3g$, we get $b - 4 = 3g - 4$. Hence, the second equation may turn into $3g - 4 = 5(g - 4)$, which implies that $3g - 4 = 5g - 20$. Thus, $2g = 16$, so $g = 8$. Substitute this value into the first equation to get $b = 3g = 3(8) = 24$. Hence, the total number of boys and girls in the room must be $b + g = 24 + 8 = 32$.

On the other hand, given $b = 3g$, we can let $b = 3k$ and $g = k$ for a third-variable introduction, and see that $3k - 4 = 5(k - 4)$ where we get $k = 8$. Since $b + g = 3k + k = 4k$, we get $b + g = 32$. When two variables appear in fractions, one may use a third-variable to simplify the given expression and solve the system of equations based on a third variable.

Worked-Example #4

At the beginning of the summer, Aiden was 160 cm tall. At the end of the summer, he measured his height again and discovered that it had increased by 5 percent. Measured in centimeters, what was the height at the end of summer?

(A) 160.8   (B) 165   (C) 168   (D) 172   (E) 175

The correct answer is (C).

Here is one suggested solution to the problem. First, we must revision what percent of increase and decrease is.

Let p be the percent of increase and P be the initial amount. Then, the new amount should be $P(1 + \frac{p}{100})$ because we are adding the newly increased amount to the original amount. In other words, $P + P(\frac{p}{100})$ is the exact paraphrase of the previous sentence.

On the other hand, let p' be the percent of decrease and P be the initial amount. Then, the new amount should be $P(1 - \frac{p'}{100})$ because we are subtracting the p' percent from the original.

What is noteworthy is that percent of increase and decrease do not stay constant in the same set-up. For example, from 10 to 11, the percent of increase is 10%. On the other hand, from 11 to 10, the percent of decrease is $9\frac{1}{11}\%$.

Another idea rooted from percent of increase and decrease is exponential growth or decay. Given an initial population P_0, if the annual growth rate is r percent, in t years, then exponential growth model tells us that the population will be

$$P_0 \left(1 + \frac{r}{100}\right)^t.$$

That being written, the original amount written in the problem is 160. The percent of increase is 5 percent, so the new height of Aiden is

$$P(1 + \frac{p}{100}) = 160(1 + \frac{5}{100}) = 160 + 160(\frac{5}{100}) = 160 + 8 = 168$$

Worked-Example #5

Consider three points A, B and C on a circle of radius 90 centimeters. The angle ACB is 40 degrees. Which of the following is the number of centimeters in the length of the minor AB?

(A) 40π (B) 45π (C) 50π (D) 55π (E) 60π

The correct answer is (A).

Here is one suggested solution to the problem. First, we must revise on circles. If two chords meet up at a point on the circle, then there exist an inscribed angle. This inscribed angle naturally forms a central angle formed by the common angle between the two radii, as shown below.

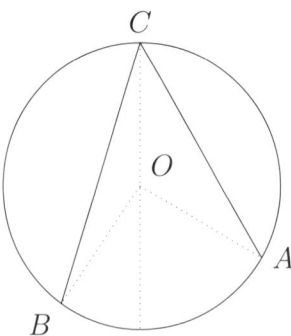

As one can see from the figure above, $m\angle AOB$ is twice $m\angle BCA$, where $\angle AOB$ is central angle and $\angle BCA$ is inscribed angle. In order to see why this is true, if $m\angle OCB = m\angle OBC = \alpha$ and $m\angle OCA = m\angle OAC = \beta$, due to isosceles triangle theorem, we get the measure of exterior angle of $\angle BOC$ as 2α and that of exterior angle of $\angle AOC$ as 2β, thanks to exterior angle theorem.

That being written, since $m\angle ACB = 40°$, we know that the associated central angle has the measure of $80°$. One more thing to revise in Geometry is that circle satisfies a weird property.

$$\text{arc length ratio} = \text{central angle ratio} = \text{sector area ratio}$$

Applying this tool to the given problem, we set

$$\frac{80°}{360°} = \frac{\text{minor AB}}{\text{circumference}} = \frac{\text{minor AB}}{180\pi}$$

Hence, the length of minor arc AC must be 40π.

Worked-Example #6

The ratio of the number of girls to the number of boys in a class of 120 students is $3:5$. At least one girl and one boy must leave the classroom so that there are equal number of boys and girls. What is the least number of people who should leave the classroom to satisfy the given condition?

(A) 2   (B) 30   (C) 31   (D) 32   (E) 33

The correct answer is (C).

Here is one suggested solution to the problem. One must label the variables - the number of boys and girls, in order to solve this problem. Let b be the number of boys and g be the number of girls in the class. Paraphrasing "a class of 120 students" and the ratio "$3:5$" into mathematical expression, we get $b + g = 120$ and $b : g = 3 : 5$.

Now, we will revise on algebra materials about proportion. For example, if $a : b = m : n$, then we can rewrite it as $\dfrac{a}{b} = \dfrac{m}{n}$. This will be an important ratio expression that can directly be translated into "slope" of a linear function. As mentioned before, we can always introduce a third variable k so that we can avoid guessing the correct answer. In other words, if $a : b = m : n$, then we may let $a = mk$ and $b = nk$ for some real number k. Applying it into our problem, we translate $b : g = 3 : 5$ into

$$\begin{cases} b = 3k \\ g = 5k \end{cases}.$$

Directly substitute these expressions into the first equation to get $b + g = 3k + 5k = (3 + 5)k = 8k = 120$. Hence, we conclude that $k = 15$. This implies that 45 girls and 75 boys.

As we read the following sentence "at least one girl and one boy must leave the classroom so that there are equal number of boys and girls," we must set the number of girls and boys leaving the class as y and x. In other words, we set $45 - y = 75 - x$, where $y \geq 1$ and $x \geq 1$. Do we need 2 equations because we have 2 variables? To this question, we may say "no" because x and y are integers. In fact, when someone tries to solve integer equations, the number of variables can be larger than the number of given equations. That being written, let's rearrange the given equation into $x - y = 30$. Since $y \geq 1$, we get $x \geq 31$. Hence, if we set $y = 1$ and $x = 31$, $45 - y = 44$ and $75 - 31 = 44$. Therefore, the least number of people leaving the classroom must be $32 (= 1 + 31)$.

Worked-Example #7

Annie was born on Wednesday. Nina was born 144 days later. On what day of the week was Nina born?

(A) Wednesday   (B) Thursday   (C) Friday   (D) Saturday   (E) Sunday

The correct answer is (E).

Here is one suggested solution to the problem. Calendar problems may involve modular arithmetic. So, what is modular arithmetic? Short answer to this deep question may involve remainder. We classify the set of integers into some finite number of classes. In order to understand modular arithmetic, we say

$$n = dq + r$$

where $0 < r < |d|$. For instance, $12 = 7(1) + 5$. This means that 5 is the remainder when 12 is divided by 7. We classify all integers into 7 different classes - a set of numbers with remainder of either 0, 1, 2, 3, 4, 5, or 6. In particular, we write $12 \equiv 5 \pmod 7$. Likewise, $n \equiv r \pmod d$.

Applying modular arithmetic in calendar, we use the fact that there are seven days in a week, so we divide the number of days into 7 to figure out how many full weeks there are and the remaining days.

In particular, if 144 days can be easily computed as 20 full weeks and 4 extra days. After 140 days from Annie's birthday, we know that it must be Wednesday. Since there are four more days to be passed since that day, we write down the following 1-to-1 corresponding list.

1. 141st day : Thursday

2. 142nd day : Friday

3. 143rd day : Saturday

4. 144th day : Sunday

Hence, Nina was born in Sunday.

Worked-Example #8

Riley is making a sundae. She must randomly choose at least one flavour of ice cream (chocolate, vanilla, or strawberry) and at least one topping (banana slices, strawberry slices, or frosted flakes). Assuming that her topping selection is independent of her flavour selection, what is the probability that she will choose a sundae with a single-flavoured ice cream with exactly one topping?

(A) $\dfrac{4}{49}$ (B) $\dfrac{5}{49}$ (C) $\dfrac{1}{7}$ (D) $\dfrac{9}{49}$ (E) $\dfrac{10}{49}$

The correct answer is (D).

Here is one suggested solution to the problem. First, this deals with the concept of "permutation allowing repetition." If we were to put distinguishable objects onto distinguishable plates, then we call such counting structure as "permutation allowing repetition." We can set up Riley's choices of flavour as the following set of choices, according to the condition laid out. For convenience, let's abbreviate chocolate, vanilla, and strawberry into C, V and S.

$$\{\{C\}, \{V\}, \{M\}, \{C, V\}, \{C, M\}, \{V, M\}, \{C, V, M\}\}$$

Likewise, if we abbreviate the toppings as B, S and F, then we get the full list of choices as

$$\{\{B\}, \{S\}, \{F\}, \{B, S\}, \{B, F\}, \{S, F\}, \{B, S, F\}\}$$

Hence, the probability that Riley chooses exactly one flavour equals $\dfrac{3}{7}$. Likewise, the probability that Riley chooses exactly one topping also equals $\dfrac{3}{7}$. Now, for two events A and B, the probability of A and B to occur at the same time is given by $P(A \text{ and } B) = P(A) \times P(B|A) = P(B) \times P(A|B)$. Normally, A and B are dependent events, i.e., the probability of A occurring when B has occurred different from that of A occurring on its own.

However, as you read along the sentences in the problem, we notice that her topping selection is independent of her flavour selection. This indicates that A and B are "independent." What does this mean? It implies that $P(A \text{ and } B) = P(A) \times P(B)$. In other words, $P(B) = P(B|A)$. More specifically, the probability of B to occur on its natural state is same as that of B to occur when A has occurred. So, the answer we want must be

$$\frac{3}{7} \times \frac{3}{7} = \frac{9}{49}.$$

Worked-Example #9

The sum of the first 100 positive integers is 5050. That is, $1+2+\cdots+99+100 = 5050$. What is the sum of the first 100 positive odd integers?

(A) 5050   (B) 10000   (C) 10050   (D) 10100   (E) 10150

The correct answer is (B).

Here is one suggested solution to the problem. In order to solve this problem, we must use arithmetic series, or sigma notation. We know that the positive odd integers in consecutive order form an arithmetic sequence. In order to solve this, we should learn about the formula for $S_n = a_1 + a_2 + \cdots + a_n$ where $\{a_n\}$ is an arithmetic sequence. This is how we deduce the sum formula for arithmetic series.

$$S_n = a_1 + a_2 + a_3 + \cdots + a_{n-1} + a_n$$
$$S_n = a_n + a_{n-1} + a_{n-2} + \cdots + a_2 + a_1$$

If we perform vertical addition, we get $2S_n = (a_1 + a_n) + (a_2 + a_{n-1}) + \cdots + (a_n + a_1)$. Since $a_1 + a_n = a_2 + a_{n-1} = a_3 + a_{n-2} = \cdots = a_{n-1} + a_2 = a_n + a_1$, we deduce the arithmetic series formula for n terms as

$$S_n = \frac{n(a_1 + a_n)}{2}.$$

That being written, we can calculate the first term as 1 and the last term as 199. Hence, the sum must be $\dfrac{100(1 + 199)}{2} = 10000$.

On the other hand, if we use sigma notation, i.e.,

$$\sum_{k=1}^{n} k = \frac{n(n+1)}{2} \qquad \sum_{k=1}^{n} k^2 = \frac{n(n+1)(2n+1)}{6} \qquad \sum_{k=1}^{n} k^3 = \left(\frac{n(n+1)}{2}\right)^2$$

we may set up the sigma notation.

$$\sum_{k=1}^{100} 2k - 1 = 2 \sum_{k=1}^{100} k - \sum_{k=1}^{100} 1$$
$$= 2 \left(\frac{100(101)}{2}\right) - 100$$
$$= 10100 - 100$$
$$= 10000$$

Worked-Example #10

> When 135 is multiplied to a positive integer n, it turns into a perfect square. Which of the following is the smallest possible value of n?
>
> (A) 3   (B) 5   (C) 15   (D) 25   (E) 35

The correct answer is (C).

Here is one suggested solution to the problem. In order to make a perfect square, we must revise on prime factorization. Any positive integer n has unique prime factorization, i.e.,

$$n = p_1^{q_1} p_2^{q_2} \cdots p_k^{q_k}$$

for different primes p_i's and non-negative integer exponents q_i's. Out of unique prime factorized forms, if exponents are even, we call such number as perfect squares. For example, $36 = 6^2 = 2^2 3^2$, or $49 = 7^2$. Although this problem does not ask these forms, the number of positive divisors of perfect squares is *odd*. We may choose to include none of the prime factors or all of the prime factors in $q_i + 1$ number of times. Since q_i is assumed to be even, we know that $q_i + 1$ is always odd.

Using this idea, let's paraphrase the first sentence into variable expressions. When 135 is multiplied to a positive integer, it turns into a perfect square. This can be written as $135n = k^2$ for some integer k. Then, we should prime-factorize 135 into the product of primes, i.e., $135 = 3^3 \cdot 5$.

Since $3^3 \cdot 5 \cdot n = k^2$, we conclude that n should have at least one 3 and one 5 and some extra perfect squares, if possible. Hence, n can be written as $n = 15x^2$ for some integer x. The main reason why $n = 3^{q_1} 5^{q_2} x^2$ is not used is because other than one 3 or one 5, these two primes must appear in even-power, which is naturally counted inside x^2.

The smallest perfect square for x^2 is 1, not 0. If we put 0, then the value of n turns into 0. Thus, we set $x^2 = 1$ and $n = 15x^2 = 15(1) = 15$.

Worked-Example #11

The number 1999 is multiplied by 1000-digit number that has all its digit equal to 1. Which of the following correctly captures the number of distinct digits in the resulting number?

(A) 2 (B) 3 (C) 4 (D) 5 (E) 6

The correct answer is (D).

Here is one suggested solution to the problem. If someone tries to multiply 1999 to a n-digit number, it shall definitely be a nightmare. How should we try to solve this type of problem? The first tool we can use is that if we multiply some integer by powers of 10, it is not so difficult for us to calculate the number. Guess what? $1999 = 2000 - 1$. In fact, multiplying 2000 would be much easier than 1999.

Now, let's perform some calculations in base cases, as though we are performing induction.

- $1111 \times 1999 = 1111 \times (2000 - 1) = 2220889$

- $11111 \times 1999 = 11111 \times (2000 - 1) = 22210889$

- $111111 \times 1999 = 111111 \times (2000 - 1) = 222110889$

- $1111111 \times 1999 = 1111 \times (2000 - 1) = 2221110889$

- $11111111 \times 1999 = 11111 \times (2000 - 1) = 22211110889$

- $111111111 \times 1999 = 111111 \times (2000 - 1) = 222111110889$

- $\vdots$

As one can check from the previous cases, digits $\{0, 1, 2, 8, 9\}$ keep appearing in the representation. Hence, we conclude that there are 5 different digits in the resulting number.

Worked-Example #12

> An isosceles trapezoid with bases 9 and 19 units and legs of 13 units has two diagonals. Which of the following is the product of the lengths of the diagonals?
>
> (A) 250   (B) 340   (C) 430   (D) 510   (E) 620

The correct answer is (B).

Here is one suggested solution to the problem. Since the problem asks us about lengths, one must think of Pythagorean Theorem. However, one may also think of isosceles trapezoid as a cyclic quadrilateral. If we focus on Pythagorean Theorem to solve the given problem, the following picture will be extremely helpful to understand how to solve the problem, providing information about the height and the diagonals.

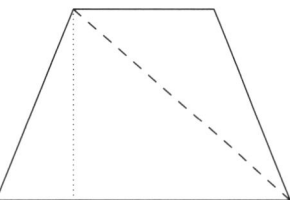

As one can check from the figure above, the height is 12 such that it forms $5 - 12 - 13$ triangle with the leg as its hypotenuse. This indicates that

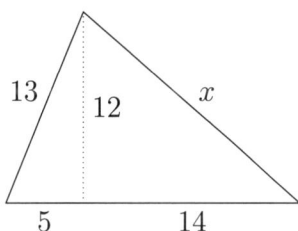

Thanks to Pythagorean Theorem, we get $x^2 = 14^2 + 12^2 = 196 + 144 = 340$. Since we are looking for the product of diagonals, which are congruent, the answer is 340.

On the other hand, if we were to use Ptolemy Theorem, due to cyclic quadrilateral, we use the following diagram.

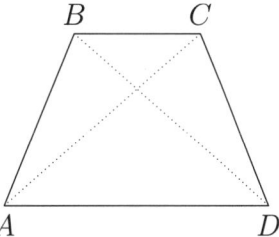

According to Ptolemy Theorem, $AB \times CD + BC \times AD = AC \times BD$. If we let $AC = BD = x$, then $13 \times 13 + 9 \times 19 = 169 + 171 = 340 = x^2$.

Worked-Example #13

What is the remainder of $10^4 - 10$, when divided by 7?

(A) 0   (B) 1   (C) 3   (D) 5   (E) 6

The correct answer is (B).

Here is one suggested solution to the problem. We can use Fermat's Little Theorem or find patterns in modular arithmetic. According to Fermat's Little Theorem,

$$a^{p-1} \equiv 1 \pmod p$$

for prime p, where a is relatively prime to p. In particular, $10^6 \equiv 1 \pmod 7$. In fact, it is easy to check that $1000 \equiv -1 \pmod 7$. Hence,

$$
\begin{aligned}
10^4 - 10 = (10^3 - 1)(10) \\
\equiv (-1 - 1)(10) \pmod 7 \\
\equiv -20 \pmod 7 \\
\equiv 1 \pmod 7
\end{aligned}
$$

On the other hand, we can find patterns in the remainders, i.e.,

$$
\begin{aligned}
10^1 &\equiv 3 \pmod 7 \\
10^2 &\equiv 2 \pmod 7 \\
10^3 &\equiv 6 \pmod 7 \\
10^4 &\equiv 4 \pmod 7 \\
10^5 &\equiv 5 \pmod 7 \\
10^6 &\equiv 1 \pmod 7
\end{aligned}
$$

We stop when 1 (mod 7) comes out because the next number will repeat with the sequence of 3, 2, 6, 4, 5 and 1. Since we are looking for $10^4 - 10 \pmod 7$, we get $4 - 3 \equiv 1 \pmod 7$.

Worked-Example #14

How many different 4-digit numbers can be obtained by using any 4 of the digits 2, 3, 7, 7, and 7?

(A) 17   (B) 18   (C) 19   (D) 20   (E) 23

The correct answer is (D).

Here is one suggested solution to the problem. The problem we face is that there are three 7s. The hard part we see in this problem is that 7s are not distinguishable.

In order to tackle this problem, we must perform casework on the number of 7s being used. Read the following question and answer.

Q. In how many ways can one 7, two 7s, or three 7s are pulled?
A. In one way each because if we say three ways, the we have considered identical-looking 7s differently. Now, we use this to perform caseworks.

1. no 7 is used : it is impossible to set up a 4-digit number without using any 7.

2. one 7 is used : it is impossible to set up a 4-digit number in this scenario.

3. two 7s are used : we must pull all 2 and 3 into the expression to arrange $\{2, 3, 7, 7\}$. There are $\frac{4!}{1!1!2!} = 12$ number of ways to arrange these digits.

4. three 7s are used : we must pull either 2 or 3 into out set $\{\bigstar, 7, 7, 7\}$.

   If $\bigstar = 2$, then there are $\frac{4!}{1!3!} = 4$ number of ways to arrange the four digits.

   On the other hand, if $\bigstar = 3$, then there are $\frac{4!}{1!3!} = 4$ number of ways to arrange the four digits. Hence, there are 8 possible ways to arrange the given digits in this scenario.

Hence, there are 20 number of ways to make a 4-digit numbers satisfying the given condition.

Worked-Example #15

> How many four-digit numbers greater than 2999 can be formed such that the product of the middle two digits exceeds 5?
>
> **(A)** 2840 **(B)** 3550 **(C)** 4260 **(D)** 4970 **(E)** 7100

The correct answer is (D).

Here is one suggested solution to the problem. This is a classic problem about digit conditions. In order to solve for digits problems, we must label the four-digit numbers as $\overline{ABCD}$. Let's write down the condition on the expressions.

1. $A \geq 3$: this implies that A is one of the digits from $\{3, 4, 5, 6, 7, 8, 9\}$.

2. $B \times C > 5$: there are two ways to solve this condition. First, we can directly count the whole set-up.

    If $B = 1$, then $C = 6, 7, 8$, and 9.

    If $B = 2$, then $C = 3, 4, 5, 6, 7, 8$, and 9.

    If $B = 3, 4$, and 5, then $C = 2, 3, 4, 5, 6, 7, 8$, and 9.

    If $B = 6, 7, 8$, and 9, then C can be anything from 1 to 9, inclusive. Hence, there are 71 pairs of (B, C) satisfying the given condition. On the other hand, we can use complementary counting. There are 100 pairs of (B, C) in total. We must eliminate the number of (B, C) satisfying $B \times C \leq 5$.

    $B \times C = 5$, then $(B, C) = (5, 1), (1, 5)$.

    $B \times C = 4$, then $(B, C) = (4, 1), (2, 2), (1, 4)$.

    $B \times C = 3$, then $(B, C) = (1, 3), (3, 1)$.

    $B \times C = 2$, then $(B, C) = (1, 2), (2, 1)$.

    $B \times C = 1$, then $(B, C) = (1, 1)$.

    $B \times C = 0$, then $(B, C) = (0, 0), (0, \bigstar)$, and $(\bigstar, 0)$ where $\bigstar \in \{1, 2, 3, 4, 5, 6, 7, 8, 9\}$. There are 29 pairs of (B, C) to eliminate. Out of 100 pairs, there are 29 pairs to eliminate. Thus, there are 71 pairs of (B, C) satisfying the given condition.

3. D can be any digit : there are 10 possible digits.

Hence, there are $4970 (= 7 \times 71 \times 10)$ number of four-digit integers satisfying the given condition.

Worked-Example #16

Consider a regular tetrahedron P with an edge of length 3 units. A polyhedron is made by cutting a regular tetrahedron with an edge of one unit from each of the four corners of the tetrahedron P. Compute the surface area of the newly made polyhedron.

(A) $4\sqrt{3}$ (B) $5\sqrt{3}$ (C) $6\sqrt{3}$ (D) $7\sqrt{3}$ (E) $8\sqrt{3}$

The correct answer is (D).

Here is one suggested solution to the problem. Let's have a look at the following figure.

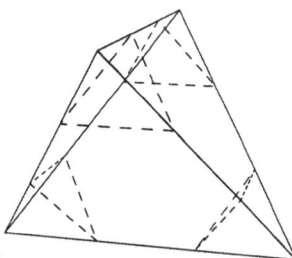

As one can see from the polyhedron, we gut four smaller regular tetrahedron away from the larger tetrahedron such that there are four hexagon faces and four equilateral triangle faces.

Each of the hexagon consists of six smaller equilateral triangle of side length 1, so its area must be $\dfrac{\sqrt{3}}{4} \times 1^2 \times 6 = \dfrac{3\sqrt{3}}{2}$. In order to understand how this happens, one must look at the following figure.

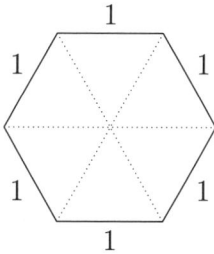

Since there are four faces in the polyhedron, the area of hexagons is $6\sqrt{2}$. On the other hand, there are four equilateral triangles of side length 1, whose area equals $\dfrac{\sqrt{3}}{4} \times 1^2$. There are four such triangles, so the area formed by four triangles is $\sqrt{3}$. The sum of all possible regions equals $7\sqrt{3}$.

Worked-Example #17

A rectangle with a width of 4 cm and a length of 18 cm can be filled with four congruent circles of radius 2. There can be a smaller circle externally tangent to two consecutive circles that is also tangent to the side of the rectangle. Which of the following correctly measures the radius of the smaller circle?

(A) $\dfrac{1}{2}$ (B) $\dfrac{1}{3}$ (C) $\dfrac{1}{4}$ (D) $\dfrac{1}{5}$ (E) $\dfrac{1}{6}$

The correct answer is (A).

Here is one suggested solution to the problem. If one sees externally tangent circles, one must connect centers, and use Pythagorean Theorem or the Law of Cosines. Here is the general set of instructions for externally tangent / internally tangent circle problems.

Step 1. Connect the centers.
Step 2. Label sides with radii.
Step 3. Set up either Pythagorean Theorem or Law of Cosines.

Let's refer to the following figure for better understanding.

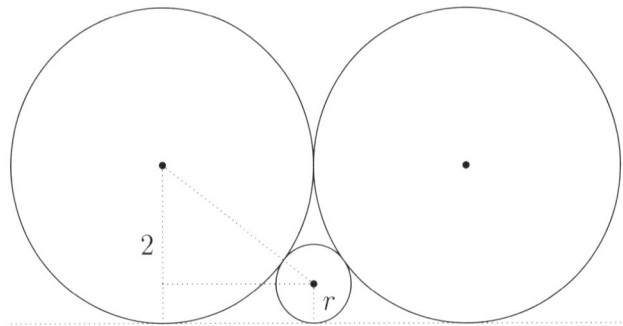

As shown in the figure above, we can easily set up Pythagorean Theorem,

$$(2 + r)^2 = (2 - r)^2 + 2^2$$
$$4 + 4r + r^2 = 4 - 4r + r^2 + 4$$
$$8r = 4$$
$$r = \frac{4}{8}$$
$$= \frac{1}{2}$$

Worked-Example #18

Aaron chooses two items for a snack. His item choices are apples, oranges, bananas, and granola bars. How many different pairs of snacks could he choose, assuming he can choose all apples, all oranges, all bananas, all granola bars, or mixed?

(A) 5   (B) 7   (C) 8   (D) 9   (E) 10

The correct answer is (E).

Here is one suggested solution to the given problem. Let's set up some equations that could express this situation. Let a, o, b and g be the number of apples, oranges, bananas, or granola bars Aaron chooses. Then, we can set up $a + o + b + g = 2$. In order to find the number of possible solutions, we lock the order by assuming $a \geq o \geq b \geq g$. Then,

$$a + o + b + g = 2$$
$$2 + 0 + 0 + 0 = 2$$
$$1 + 1 + 0 + 0 = 2$$

There are two possible types of solutions we may get - same types or mixed types. Let's investigate a bit more about each solution.

1. $(a, o, b, g) = (2, 0, 0, 0)$: The original assumption $a \geq o \geq b \geq g$ must be discarded, so we permute all possible cases as $(a, o, b, g) = (2, 0, 0, 0)$, $(0, 2, 0, 0)$, $(0, 0, 2, 0)$, and $(0, 0, 0, 2)$. There are four possible quadruples, which can also be computed as $\dfrac{4!}{1!3!} = 4$.

2. $(a, o, b, g) = (1, 1, 0, 0)$: Discarding the original assumption, we must permute the four digits 1, 1, 0, and 0. Hence, we get

$$a + o + b + g = 1 + 1 + 0 + 0$$
$$= 1 + 0 + 1 + 0$$
$$= 1 + 0 + 0 + 1$$
$$= 0 + 1 + 1 + 0$$
$$= 0 + 1 + 0 + 1$$
$$= 0 + 0 + 1 + 1$$

There are six possible quadruples, which can also be computed as $\dfrac{4!}{2!2!} = 6$.

Hence, there are 10 different number of ways for Aaron to buy two items.

Worked-Example #19

Which of the following correctly measures the number of positive three-digit integers whose sum of digits is even?

(A) 360 (B) 450 (C) 500 (D) 540 (E) 600

The correct answer is (B).

Here is one suggested solution to the given problem. First, label a three-digit positive integer as $\overline{abc}$, where $a \neq 0$. We may perform casework on a.

1. $a = 1 : b + c$ is odd. In other words, (b, c) is either (even,odd) or (odd,even).

2. $a = 2 : b + c$ is even. In other words, (b, c) is either (even,even) or (odd,odd).

3. $a = 3 : b + c$ is odd. In other words, (b, c) is either (even,odd) or (odd,even).

4. $a = 4 : b + c$ is even. In other words, (b, c) is either (even,even) or (odd,odd).

5. $a = 5 : b + c$ is odd. In other words, (b, c) is either (even,odd) or (odd,even).

6. $a = 6 : b + c$ is even. In other words, (b, c) is either (even,even) or (odd,odd).

7. $a = 7 : b + c$ is odd. In other words, (b, c) is either (even,odd) or (odd,even).

8. $a = 8 : b + c$ is even. In other words, (b, c) is either (even,even) or (odd,odd).

9. $a = 9 : b + c$ is odd. In other words, (b, c) is either (even,odd) or (odd,even).

As one can see from the casework above, when a is odd, then we have equal number of pairs of (b, c). Likewise, when a is even, we also have equal number of pairs of (b, c). Let's find out these numbers more in detail.

1. $b + c$ is odd : if (b, c)=(even,odd), there are 25 pairs of (b, c); if (b, c)=(odd,even), there are 25 pairs of (b, c). Hence, there are 50 pairs of (b, c).

2. $b + c$ is even : if (b, c)=(even,even), there are 25 pairs of (b, c); if (b, c)=(odd,odd), there are 25 pairs of (b, c). Hence, there are 50 pairs of (b, c).

Since each case produces 50 pairs of (b, c), we conclude that there are 450 triples of (a, b, c) satisfying the original condition.

Worked-Example #20

> The mean of a set of six integers is 10. If the number 25 is removed from the
> set, the mean of the remaining numbers is
>
> (A) 6   (B) 7   (C) 8   (D) 9   (E) 10

The correct answer is (B).

Here is one suggested solution to the given problem. First, revise on mean, median and mode. Mean is the average of data values in the given set. Median is the middle value of the given set in increasing order. Mode is the most frequent data-value in the given data set.

That being written, let's label all these information in detail. "A set of six integers" can be written as $\{x_1, x_2, x_3, x_4, x_5, x_6\}$. According to the first sentence, we can write down the equation

$$\frac{x_1 + x_2 + x_3 + x_4 + x_5 + x_6}{6} = 10$$

Hence, $x_1 + x_2 + x_3 + x_4 + x_5 + x_6 = 60$. Without loss of generality, assume that $x_6 = 25$. Since we take out x_6 from the set, we get

$$
\begin{aligned}
x_1 + x_2 + x_3 + x_4 + x_5 &= 60 - x_6 \\
&= 60 - 25 \\
&= 35.
\end{aligned}
$$

The mean of the remaining numbers must be

$$\frac{x_1 + x_2 + x_3 + x_4 + x_5}{5} = \frac{35}{5} = 7$$

Worked-Example #21

How many positive integers between 10 and 2023 are divisible by 3 and have all of their digits the same?

(A) 3 (B) 6 (C) 9 (D) 12 (E) 48

The correct answer is (D).

Here is one suggested solution to the given problem. As we investigate its condition, we notice that performing casework will suffice. Remember that there are two main rules to follow for case enumerations - comprehensively and exhaustively.

The first case is when we have two digit numbers. Let's label a two-digit number as $\overline{aa}$. Then, we can write either $a + a \equiv 0 \pmod 3$ or $a + a = 3, 6, 9, 12, 15,$ or 18. Since $2a$ is an even number, we get $2a = 6, 12$ or 18. This implies that $33, 66$ and 99 are two-digit numbers that satisfy the given condition.

Second, let $\overline{aaa}$ be a three-digit number that satisfies the given condition. Then, we can write either $a + a + a \equiv 0 \pmod 3$ or $a + a + a = 3a = 3, 6, 9, 12, 15, 18, 21, 24,$ and 27. Thus, $a = 1, 2, 3, 4, 5, 6, 7, 8$ and 9. There are 9 three-digit numbers that satisfy the given condition, i.e., $111, 222, 333, 444, 555, 666, 777, 888,$ and 999.

Third, let $\overline{aaaa}$ be a four-digit number that satisfies the given condition. Then, we can write either $a + a + a + a \equiv 4a \equiv 0 \pmod 3$. Unlike the previous two cases, let's solve the modular equation.

$$4a \equiv 0 \pmod 3$$
$$1a \equiv 0 \pmod 3$$
$$a \equiv 0 \pmod 3$$

This implies that a can be either $0, 3, 6,$ or 9. Then, four-digit numbers can be written as $0000, 3333, 6666,$ or 9999. The first one makes no sense, so we discard it. The rest numbers are not in the constraints, so we conclude there is no four-digit positive integer satisfying the given condition.

Hence, we have 12 positive integers in total.

Worked-Example #22

In a car market, 40% of the cars are blue and 12% of the blue cars have two doors. What is the probability that a buyer would buy a blue car with two doors?

(A) 48 percent (B) 4.8 percent (C) 32 percent (D) 3.2 percent (E) 1.2 percent

The correct answer is (B).

Here is one suggested solution to the given problem. First, we must review on the definition of probability of compound events.

$$p(A \cap B) = p(A) \times p(B|A) = p(B) \times p(A|B)$$

where $p(B|A)$ is the probability of B happening, after A has occurred. It does not matter whether A or B happens first. What matters is the conditional probability that follows. Algebraic manipulation shows that

- $p(A|B) = \dfrac{p(A \cap B)}{p(B)}$: the probability of A happening, given that B has occurred is the proportion of A within B.

- $p(B|A) = \dfrac{p(B \cap A)}{p(A)}$: similarly, the probability of B happening, given that A has occurred is the proportion of B within A.

That being written, the probability that a buyer would buy a blue car with two doors can be computed as

$$p(\text{blue} \cap \text{two doors}) = p(\text{blue}) \times p(\text{two doors}|\text{blue}) = 0.4 \times 0.12 = 0.048$$

Hence, the probability is 4.8 percent.

Worked-Example #23

Ann chooses one diagonal from a regular octagon. Ben chooses another diagonal from the same polygon. What is the probability that they choose two diagonals of the same length?

(A) $\dfrac{33}{95}$ (B) $\dfrac{32}{95}$ (C) $\dfrac{31}{95}$ (D) $\dfrac{6}{19}$ (E) $\dfrac{29}{95}$

The correct answer is (C).

Here is one suggested solution to the given problem. There are 20 diagonals formed inside a regular octagon. In order to find out the number of diagonals, we first connect two vertices together to find out $\dfrac{8 \times 7}{2} = 28$ number of edges. However, we subtract 8 edges that are not diagonals. Now, we can easily classify all diagonals of regular octagon as shown in the following figures.

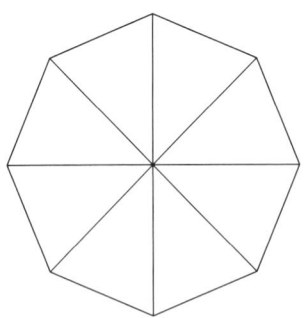

4 longest diagonals

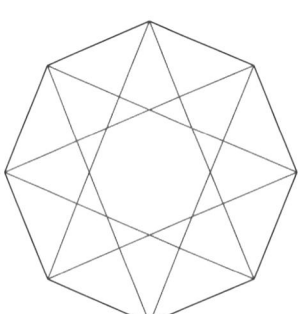

8 intermediate diagonals

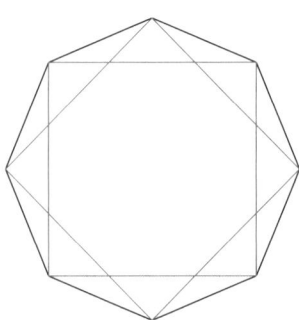

8 shortest diagonals

According to the given condition, we compute the probabilities when Ann and Ben chooses diagonals from each respective cases.

1. Ann and Ben choosing longest diagonals together : $\dfrac{4}{20} \times \dfrac{3}{19} = \dfrac{3}{95}$.

2. Ann and Ben choosing intermediate diagonals together : $\dfrac{8}{20} \times \dfrac{7}{19} = \dfrac{14}{95}$.

3. Ann and Ben choosing shortest diagonals together : $\dfrac{8}{20} \times \dfrac{7}{19} = \dfrac{14}{95}$.

Hence, the probability that they choose diagonals of same length equals

$$\frac{3}{95} + \frac{14}{95} + \frac{14}{95} = \frac{31}{95}.$$

Worked-Example #24

> If two distinct numbers are selected at random from the first 11 prime numbers, what is the probability that their sum is an even number?
> (A) $\dfrac{7}{11}$ (B) $\dfrac{8}{11}$ (C) $\dfrac{9}{11}$ (D) $\dfrac{10}{11}$ (E) 1

The correct answer is (C).

Here is one suggested solution to the given problem. Let's first list out the first 11 prime numbers as $\{2, 3, 5, 7, 11, 13, 17, 19, 23, 29\}$. In order to see whether the sum is an even number, we must think about casework as

- even + even = even

- even + odd = odd

- odd + even = odd

- odd + odd = even

The first case is impossible, since there is only one even prime number in the list. The last case is what we want, so we compute the probability using the principle of multiplication as

$$\frac{10}{11} \times \frac{9}{10} = \frac{9}{11}$$

Since odd primes are indistinct kinds, we do not multiply by extra orders that may have been formed by rearranging odd primes.

Here is a quick revision on equal kinds and different kinds in probability. It all depends on contexts, but we may understand the multiplication principle of probability in the following example. For example, let there be three male dogs and four female dogs. Then,

1. Probability of choosing two male dogs : $\dfrac{\dbinom{3}{2}}{\dbinom{7}{2}} = \dfrac{3}{7} \times \dfrac{2}{6}$, for they are of same kinds.

2. Probability of choosing one male dog and one female dog : $\dfrac{\dbinom{3}{1}\dbinom{4}{1}}{\dbinom{7}{2}} = \dfrac{3}{7} \times \dfrac{4}{6} \times 2!$, for they are of different kinds.

Worked-Example #25

Given a positive two-digit integer with the sum of the two digits equal to 6, what is the probability that one of the digits is greater than 4?

(A) $\frac{1}{6}$ (B) $\frac{1}{3}$ (C) $\frac{1}{2}$ (D) $\frac{5}{6}$ (E) 1

The correct answer is (C).

Here is one suggested solution to the given problem. First, we label a positive two-digit numbers as $\overline{AB}$. According to the condition, $A + B = 6$. We can write down all possible cases such that

$$A + B = 6$$
$$6 + 0 = 6$$
$$5 + 1 = 6$$
$$4 + 2 = 6$$
$$3 + 3 = 6$$
$$2 + 4 = 6$$
$$1 + 5 = 6$$

Out of 6 ordered pairs, we must check that one of the digits must be greater than 4. This means that $(A, B) = (6, 0), (5, 1)$, and $(1, 5)$. Hence, there are 3 pairs of (A, B) that satisfy the given condition. Therefore, the probability that one of the digits is greater than 4 is $\frac{3}{6}\left(=\frac{1}{2}\right)$.

"Dream big and dare to fail."

2

2.1 Problem Set

Problem 1.
Keywords: De Morgan's Law, Principle of Inclusion and Exclusion, Derangement

In how many ways can one distribute four unique keys for four different lockers so that none of the lockers will be unlocked?

(A) 8

(B) 9

(C) 10

(D) 11

(E) 12

Problem 2.
Keywords: Adjacency, Repeated Letters, Permutation with Restriction

Using all of the written letters in $SCHOOLS$, in how many ways can the letters be arranged such that none of the repeating letters is adjacent?

(A) 640

(B) 650

(C) 660

(D) 670

(E) 680

Problem 3.
Keywords: De Morgan's Law, Legendre Function, Floor Function

In how many integers between 1 and 100 such that it is not divisible by 2 nor 5?

(A) 40

(B) 50

(C) 60

(D) 70

(E) 80

Problem 4.

Keywords: Finite Geometric Series, One-to-one Correspondence

The sum $1 + 1/2 + 1/4 + ... + 1/2^{12}$ can be written as m/n where m and n are relatively prime positive integers. Find the number of integers exclusively between m and n.

(A) 4092

(B) 4093

(C) 4094

(D) 4095

(E) 4096

Problem 5.

Keywords: Fixed Order, Combination vs. Permutation

There are six cards labeled with 1, 2, 3, X, Y, and Z. If all alphabets must be arranged in alphabetical order and all integers in increasing order, in how many ways can six cards be arranged from left to right?

(A) 16

(B) 17

(C) 18

(D) 19

(E) 20

Problem 6.

Keywords: Casework, Difference between Counting and Probability

When two of the eight cards A, B, C, C, C, C, D, and E are randomly selected to form a two-letter word, how many distinct two-letter words can be formed?

(A) 17

(B) 19

(C) 21

(D) 23

(E) 25

Problem 7.

Keywords: De Morgan's Law, Legendre Function, Floor Function

How many positive four digit integers can be formed if all of the four digits 2, 3, 5, and 7 are used and the resulting four-digit number is divisible by 4?

(A) 6

(B) 7

(C) 8

(D) 9

(E) 10

Problem 8.

Keywords: Casework, Permutation with Repeated Letters

How many positive 11-digit integers can be formed using five 2s and six 5s such that the resulting number is divisible by 5?

(A) 246

(B) 248

(C) 250

(D) 252

(E) 254

Problem 9.

Keywords: Constructive Counting, Principle of Multiplication in Counting

If there are three adults and four children to be seated in a row of chairs such that all children must be seated apart, in how many ways can these seven people be seated?

(A) 36

(B) 72

(C) 108

(D) 144

(E) 196

Problem 10.

Keywords: Casework, Divisibility

When two different dice are rolled, how many ways are there in which the product of the two eyes is divisible by 2, not by 4?

(A) 10

(B) 12

(C) 14

(D) 16

(E) 18

Problem 11.

Keywords: Labeling, Digits

In how many four-digit positive integers have their product of digits *odd*?

(A) 484

(B) 529

(C) 576

(D) 625

(E) 676

Problem 12.

Keywords: Labeling, Digits, Complementary Counting

In how many five-digit positive integers have their product of digits *even*?

(A) 73125

(B) 76585

(C) 82500

(D) 86875

(E) 90000

2.2 Solution Manual

1. **(B)** 9

Let A be the case when the first key unlocks the first locker, B be the case when the second key unlocks the second locker, C be the case when the third key unlocks the third locker, and D be the case when the fourth key unlocks the fourth locker.

We are looking for $n(A^c \cap B^c \cap C^c \cap D^c)$. Using De Morgan's Law, we compute $n((A \cup B \cup C \cup D)^c)$. Let U be the universal set. Hence, we are looking for $n(U) - n(A \cup B \cup C \cup D)$. Without loss of generality, we assume that the first key unlocks the first locker. Then, there are $3!$ number of ways to arrange three remaining keys to three remaining lockers. This implies that $n(A) = n(B) = n(C) = n(D) = 3! = 6$. On the other hand, if we assume that the first key unlocks the first locker and the second key unlocks the second locker. Then, there are $2!$ number of ways to arrange two remaining keys to two remaining lockers. Thus, $n(A \cap B) = n(A \cap C) = n(A \cap D) = \cdots = n(C \cap D) = 2$.

Now, if we assume three keys unlock the three lockers, then we have 1 way to send the remaining key to remaining locker. Thus, $n(A \cap B \cap C) = \cdots = n(B \cap C \cap D) = 1$. Lastly, if all four keys unlock their own lockers, we must count it as once. Thus, by the principle of inclusion and exclusion, we get

$$
\begin{aligned}
4! - (4 \cdot 3! - 6 \cdot 2! + 4 \cdot 1! - 1 \cdot 0!) &= 24 - (24 - 12 + 4 - 1) \\
&= 24 - 24 + 12 - 4 + 1 \\
&= 12 - 4 + 1 \\
&= 9
\end{aligned}
$$

2. **(C)** 660

Let A be the case when two Ss are adjacent. Likewise, let B be the case when two Os are adjacent. By De Morgan's Law, $A^c \cap B^c = (A \cup B)^c$. First, we may compute $n(A)$ by placing two Ss into one bundle. Then, the arrangement of (SS), C, H, O, O and L can be computed as $\frac{6!}{2!}$. Likewise, we may compute $n(B)$ by placing two Os into one bundle. Then, the arrangement of (OO), C, H, S, S and L can be computed as $\frac{6!}{2!}$. On the other hand, the intersection of A and B can be computed by placing two Ss into one bundle and two Os into another bundle. Then, the arrangement of (SS), (OO), C, H and L can be computed as $5!$.

Therefore,

$$\frac{7!}{2!2!} - \left(\frac{6!}{2!} + \frac{6!}{2!} - 5!\right) = 1260 - (360 + 360 - 120)$$
$$= 1260 - 600$$
$$= 660$$

3. **(A)** 40

Let A be the set of multiples of 2 between 1 and 100. Let B be the set of multiples of 5 between 1 and 100. If U is the set of integers between 1 and 100, then the set of integers not divisible by 2 nor 5 can be computed as $n(A^c \cap B^c)$. By De Morgan's Law, we must compute $n(A \cup B)$. First, $n(A)$ can be computed by setting $1 < 2k < 100$ for some integer k. Since $0.5 < k < 50$, we get $k \in \{1, 2, 3, \cdots, 49\}$, implying that $n(A) = 49$. Likewise, $n(B)$ can be computed by setting $1 < 5k < 100$ for some integer k. Since $0.2 < k < 20$, we get $k \in \{1, 2, 3, \cdots, 19\}$, implying that $n(B) = 19$. Lastly, $n(A \cap B)$ can be computed by setting $1 < 10k < 100$ for some integer k. This means that $n(A \cap B) = 9$. Using the principle of inclusion and exclusion,

$$n(A \cup B) = n(A) + n(B) - n(A \cap B)$$
$$= 49 + 19 - 9$$
$$= 59$$

Since $n(U) = 99$, we get $n(A^c \cap B^c) = 99 - 59 = 40$.

4. **(C)** 4094

$$\frac{2^{12} + 2^{11} + \cdots + 2^1 + 1}{2^{12}} = \frac{2^{13} - 1}{2^{12}}$$

It is not difficult to see that $2^{12} + 2^{11} + 2^{10} + \cdots + 1 = 2^{13} - 1$. Let S be the sum of powers of 2 from 1 to 2^{12}. Then,

$$S = 1 + 2 + 2^2 + \cdots + 2^{11} + 2^{12}$$
$$2S = 2 + 2^2 + 2^3 + \cdots + 2^{12} + 2^{13}$$

Hence $2S - S = S = 2^{13} - 1$. Thus, we are looking for 1-to-1 correspondence principle to count the number of integers between 2^{12} and $2^{13} - 1$, exclusive. We must count the integers ranging from $2^{12} + 1$ to $2^{13} - 2$ by computing $(2^{13} - 2) - (2^{12} + 1) + 1$, which is equal to $2^{13} - 2^{12} - 2 = 2^{12} - 2 = 4096 - 2 = 4094$.

5. (E) 20

The problem states that letters must be arranged alphabetically, numbers in increasing order. Normally, the total number of arrangements of three letters and three integers must be $6! = 720$. However, X, Y, and Z must be arranged in (X, Y, Z). In other words, all possible arrangements of X, Y, and Z must be counted as one arrangement (X, Y, Z). In particular, $\{(X, Y, Z), (X, Z, Y), (Y, X, Z), (Y, Z, X), (Z, X, Y), (Z, Y, X)\}$ must be reduced into (X, Y, Z).

Likewise, 1, 2, and 3 must be arranged in $(1, 2, 3)$. All possible arrangements of 123 can be written as 123, 132, 213, 231, 312, and 321. Hence, these six arrangements must be reduced into 123. This indicates that we must get rid of overcounts by dividing 720 by two 6s. Hence, the answer must be

$$\frac{6!}{3!3!} = \frac{720}{6 \cdot 6} = 20$$

6. (C) 21

We perform casework on the number of Cs that appear in card selections. Since we are pick up two cards for arrangements, we begin finding the possible number of Cs that could appear. We have three possible cases : no C selected, one C selected, and two Cs selected.

First, we assume that there is no C selected. Then, we must pick up and arrange two cards from $\{A, B, D, E\}$. This must result in 12 possible 2-card arrangements, i.e., AB, AD, AE, BA, BD, BE, DA, DB, DE, EA, EB, and ED.

Second, we assume there is one C selected. Then, we must pick up one card from $\{A, B, D, E\}$. Since there are two places for C to be arranged and four ways to pick up one card from $\{A, B, D, E\}$, we have 8 possible 2-card arrangements, i.e., CA, CB, CD, CE, AC, BC, DC, and EC.

Last, we assume there are two Cs selected. Then, there is only one arrangement of two Cs in two places, i.e., CC. Therefore, we conclude that there are $21 (= 12 + 8 + 1)$ number of arrangements of 2-cards satisfying the given condition.

7. (A) 6

Divisibility by 4 can be tested by whether last two digits are divisible by 4. This can easily shown by setting up the following expression $n = 100q + r$ for $0 \le r < 100$. It is clear that 100 is already divisible by 4, so if r is divisible by 4, the given number n must be divisible by 4.

Let $\overline{ABCD}$ be a 4-digit number formed by using 2, 3, 5, and 7 exactly once. Then, we may get $\overline{CD}$ as 23, 25, 27, 32, 35, 37, 52, 53, 57, 72, 73, and 75. In order for the last two digits to be divisible by 4, we must ensure that the number must be even. Since we have 32, 52, and 72 as the only even numbers, let's test whether they are divisible by 4.

First, 32 is divisible by 4. Hence, $\overline{AB32}$ can be written as 5732 or 7532. Second, 52 is divisible by 4. Hence, $\overline{AB52}$ can be written as 3752 or 7352. Third, 72 is divisible by 4. Thus, $\overline{AB72}$ can be written as 3572 or 5372. In total, there are 6 four-digit numbers divisible by 4.

8. **(D)** 252
Since last digit must be 5, we know that there are five 2s and five 5s to arrange in the other digit places. In short, there are

$$\frac{10!}{5!5!} = \frac{10 \cdot 9 \cdot 8 \cdot 7 \cdot 6}{5 \cdot 4 \cdot 3 \cdot 2 \cdot 1} = 252$$

number of arrangements of 11 digits such that the number is divisible by 5.

9. **(D)** 144
Testing few cases, we get $CACACAC$ is the only possible arrangement that all children are seated apart. Hence, we must arrange four children in four Cs and three adults in three As. There are 4! ways to arrange four children and 3! ways to arrange three adults. Hence, there are $144(= 24 \times 6 = 4! \times 3!)$ ways to arrange seven people satisfying the given condition.

10. **(B)** 12
If the product of eyes is divisible by 2, but not by 4, this indicates that there is only one multiple of 2 in both eyes. Hence, let x_1, x_2 be the eye-value that comes up in the 1st and 2nd die, respectively. It can be easily reasoned that there are two possible cases to work on.

First, if x_1 is a multiple of 2 not divisible by 4, then x_2 must be either 1, 3 or 5. Hence, $x_1 \in \{2, 6\}$ and $x_2 \in \{1, 3, 5\}$. This implies that there are $6(= 2 \times 3)$ possible cases for the product of two eyes divisible by 2.

Second, if x_2 is a multiple of 2 not divisible by 4, then x_1 must be either 1, 3, or 5. Hence, $x_2 \in \{2, 6\}$ and $x_1 \in \{1, 3, 5\}$. This means there are $6(= 3 \times 2)$ possible cases for the product of two eyes divisible by 2.

Hence, there are 12 total ways to roll two dice such that the product of two eyes is divisible by 2, not by 4.

11. (D) 625

Let $\overline{abcd}$ be a four-digit positive integers. Then, we may write down

1. $a \in \{1, 2, 3, 4, 5, 6, 7, 8, 9\}$, so there are 9 possible cases for a.

2. $b, c, d \in \{0, 1, 2, 3, 4, 5, 6, 7, 8, 9\}$, so there are 10 possible cases for b, c, and d, respectively.

Hence, there are 9000 number of four-digit positive integers. Since the product of all digits must be odd, a, b, c, and d are all odd. This implies that $a, b, c, d \in \{1, 3, 5, 7, 9\}$. Hence, there are $5^4 = 625$ number of four-digit positive integers whose product of digits is odd.

12. (D) 86875

Let $\overline{abcde}$ be a five-digit positive integers. Similar to the problem 11, we have 90000 number of 5-digit positive integers. Since the product of digits must be even, we get rid of the number of integers whose product of digits is odd.

Hence, in order for $\overline{abcde}$ to have its product of digits odd, we get $a, b, c, d, e \in \{1, 3, 5, 7, 9\}$. Thus, there are $5^5 (= 3125)$ number of five-digit positive integers whose product of digits is odd. Therefore, the answer we want must be the difference between 90000 and 3125, which is 86875.

Designed and Tailored for
Your Successful Journey on Competition Math

" Your only limit is your mind; push past it and achieve greatness."

3.1   Problem Set

Problem 13.
Keywords: Constructive Counting, Nonadjacency

If three freshmen, four sophomores, and two juniors are to be seated in a row, determine the total number of ways to arrange all nine students such that all freshmen and juniors are apart.

(A) 1810

(B) 2210

(C) 2440

(D) 2880

(E) 2960

Problem 14.
Keywords: Permutation with Restriction, Digits, Number of Divisors

If the administrator of *Xplosive Math Meet* ensures that the serial number in 6-digits must not start with 0 nor end with 0, the number of all different serial numbers that can be formed is N. Which of the following is the number of positive divisors of N?

(A) 96

(B) 100

(C) 114

(D) 121

(E) 125

Problem 15.
Keywords: Constructive Counting, Principle of Multiplication in Counting

A family of five must ride on a SUV where there are two front seats and three back seats. If a driver must be either mother or father, and one of the parents must go in the back seats, in how many different ways can they take a ride?

(A) 12

(B) 18

(C) 24

(D) 36

(E) 48

Problem 16.

Keywords: Principle of Multiplication in Counting, Permutation allowing Repetition

One day, three athletes went to a gym. Each athlete must follow one of the routines - squat session, deadlift session, or benchpress session. In how many ways can they choose routines for the workout?

(A) 9

(B) 18

(C) 27

(D) 36

(E) 45

Problem 17.

Keywords: Constructive Counting, Casework, Principle of Multiplication in Counting

Another day, three athletes went to the gym. Each athlete must follow one of the routines - squat session, deadlift session, or benchpress session. If two athletes must share the session, while the remaining athlete should do different one, in how many different ways can they choose routines for the workout? (Hint: you must choose which two athletes are going to workout together as well.)

(A) 12

(B) 15

(C) 18

(D) 21

(E) 24

Problem 18.

Keywords: Overcounts, Circular Permutation

In how many ways can all edges of a square be colored using *all four colors* - blue, green, purple, and yellow, if a rotated figure is considered all equivalent?

(A) 6

(B) 7

(C) 8

(D) 9

(E) 10

Problem 19.

Keywords: Overcounts, Circular Permutation

In how many ways can all edges of an equilateral triangle be colored using all three colors - blue, green, and purple, assuming that two configurations are considered indistinct if rotated to be equivalent?

(A) 1

(B) 2

(C) 3

(D) 4

(E) 5

Problem 20.

Keywords: Casework, Overcounts, Circular Permutation, Principle of Multiplication in Counting

In how many ways can all vertices of an equilateral triangle be colored using *at most* three colors - blue, green, and purple, assuming that two configurations are considered indistinct if rotated to be equivalent (Hint: one may use the same colors multiple times for this problem.)

(A) 10

(B) 11

(C) 12

(D) 13

(E) 14

Problem 21.

Keywords: Constructive Counting, Principle of Multiplication in Counting

If Abbie, Benny, Chenny, and Danny went to a convenience store to buy snacks, where it sells different types of snacks - candy, icecream, bubble-gum, and chocolate-bar. If there are two kinds of candy, four kinds of icecream, three kinds of bubble-gum, and three kinds of chocolate-bar, and everyone should choose one snack of different types, in how many ways can they buy snacks?

(A) 1575

(B) 1625

(C) 1728

(D) 1936

(E) 2002

Problem 22.

Keywords: Diophantine Equation, Modular Equation, Casework

For non-negative integer pairs (m, n), determine the total number of pairs (m, n) satisfying $5m + 4n = 1000$.

(A) 50

(B) 51

(C) 52

(D) 53

(E) 54

Problem 23.

Keywords: Casework, Partition of Natural Numbers - Locking the Order

A fair die is tossed three times in a row. In how many ways will the sum of the top-face values be either 3, 6, or 9?

(A) 36

(B) 45

(C) 54

(D) 60

(E) 66

Problem 24.

Keywords: One-to-one Correspondence, Casework

Out of all three-digit positive integers, which of the following correctly counts the number of 1s in their digits?

(A) 271

(B) 280

(C) 300

(D) 325

(E) 400

3.2   Solution Manual

13. (D) 2880

Let S, F, and J be sophomore, freshman, and junior, such that there are four Ss, three Fs and two Js for grade-levels. We know that all students are distinguishable, but we have to make sure that freshmen and juniors must be non-adjacent to one another. Hence, on the checkmarks in $\checkmark S \checkmark S \checkmark S \checkmark S \checkmark$, we may send three Fs and two Js in $5!$ number of ways. Since there are $4!$ number of ways to arrange all sophomores, the answer must be $5! \times 4! = 120 \times 24 = 2880$.

14. (E) 125

Let $\overline{abcdef}$ be a six-digit serial number for *Xplosive Math Meet*. Since a and f cannot be 0, according to the given problem, we get
$N = 9 \times 9 \times 10^4 = 81 \times 10^4 = 3^4 \times 2^4 \times 5^4$. The number of positive divisors of N can be found by counting the number of possible divisors of 3^4, 2^4 and 5^4.

Divisors of 3^4 come from $\{3^0, 3^1, 3^2, 3^3, 3^4\}$. Similarly, divisors of 2^4 come from $\{2^0, 2^1, 2^2, 2^3, 2^4\}$. Lastly, divisors of 5^4 come from $\{5^0, 5^1, 5^2, 5^3, 5^4\}$. Hence, there are $5^3 (= 125)$ number of divisors of N.

15. (D) 36

First, choose a driver from {father, mother} in 2 ways. Without loss of generality, assume that the driver is father. Then, mother can choose one of the back seats in 3 ways. In the remaining three seats, other people must choose their seats in $3!$ number of ways. Hence, they may take a ride in $2 \times 3 \times 3! = 36$ number of ways.

16. (C) 27

Since there are three athletes, we call them A_1, A_2, and A_3. For A_1, there are three possible workout routines he or she can choose that day. This works out exactly the same way for A_2 and A_3. Hence, they can choose their routines in $3^3 (= 27)$ number of ways.

17. (C) 18

First, we must choose two athletes who will perform partner workout. Out of $\{A_1, A_2, A_3\}$, we can lay out all possibilities as $(A_1, (A_2, A_3))$, $(A_2, (A_1, A_3))$, $(A_3, (A_1, A_2))$.

Without loss of generality, let's assume that A_1 workouts on his or her own. Let A_1 choose one of the routines first, in 3 different ways. Then, A_2 and A_3 only have 2 possible routines to choose. Hence, they choose routines for the workout in $3 \times 3 \times 2 = 18$ different ways.

18. (A) 6

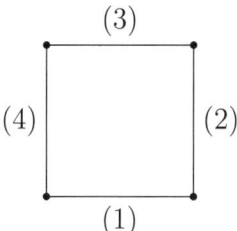

Notice that under rotation, $((1), (2), (3), (4))$ is indistinct from $((2), (3), (4), (1))$, $((3), (4), (1), (2))$, and $((4), (1), (2), (3))$. In other words, one coloring comes out four number of times when we count. Since there are four colors - blue, green, purple, and yellow - to paint on (1), (2), (3), and (4), there are $4!(= 24)$ number of ways to arrange all four colors. Since there are three overlaps per each coloring, all edges of a square can be colored using four colors in $\dfrac{24}{4} = 6$ different ways.

19. (B) 2

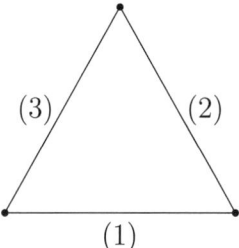

In $((1), (2), (3))$, we arrange three colors in $3!$ number of ways. Since there are two overlaps per one coloring, all edges of an equilateral triangle can be colored in $\dfrac{3!}{3} = 2$ different ways.

20. (B) 11

We should perform casework on the number of colors used for vertices. First, if we use one color, then three different triangles are formed. Second, if we use two colors, we must decide which color we use twice, in 3 different ways, and decide which color we use once, in 2 different ways. There are 6 different triangles formed using two different colors. Lastly, if we use three colors, this is the same case as the previous problem, so there are 2 different triangles. In fact, the following visual information will help you figure out the differences.

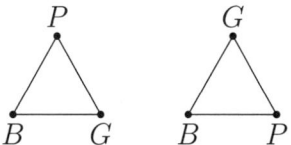

As one can see from the figures above, however one rotates, one cannot produce the other one, unless someone flips the figure. Since *flip* is not allowed in this problem, we consider these two different. Hence, adding all up, all vertices of an equilateral triangle can be colored in 11 number of ways, satisfying the given condition.

21. (C) 1728

Let (A, B, C, D) be a 4-tuple representing Abbie, Benny, Chenny, and Danny. First, they must choose all different types of snacks in 4! different ways. Without loss of generality, assume that Abbie chooses candy, Benny ice-cream, Chenny bubble-gum, and Danny chocolate-bar. Second, Abbie has 2 choices; Benny has 4 choices; Chenny has 3 choices; Danny has 3 choices. Thanks to the principle of multiplication in counting, they may buy snacks in

$$4! \times 2 \times 4 \times 3 \times 3 = 1728$$

number of ways.

22. (B) 51

For $5m + 4n = 1000$, one can find one obvious solution $(200, 0)$. The next solution for this Diophantine equation is $(196, 5)$. One may find all solutions all the way upto $(0, 250)$. Since these are linearly changing, we focus on the y-values of all solutions ranging from 0 to 250. It starts from 0, goes up by 5, and ends at 250. Let such value be $5k$. Then, $0 = 5(0), 5 = 5(1), \cdots, 250 = 5(50)$. Hence, there are 51 possible values of y. Since x-value depends on y-value, in linear fashion, we conclude that there are 51 pairs of (m, n) satisfying $5m + 4n = 1000$.

23. (A) 36

Let x, y, and z be the eye-value that appears in each die, respectively. We must solve for the number of distinct triples (x, y, z) satisfying $x + y + z = 3$, 6, and 9.

First, in order to solve $x + y + z = 3$, we assume $x \geq y \geq z$. Then, $(x, y, z) = (1, 1, 1)$. Getting rid of the original assumption of $x \geq y \geq z$, we still have 1 triple.

Second, in order to solve $x + y + z = 6$, we assume $x \geq y \geq z$. Then,

$$x + y + z = 6$$
$$4 + 1 + 1 = 6$$
$$3 + 2 + 1 = 6$$
$$2 + 2 + 2 = 6$$

Here, $(4, 1, 1)$ can be rearranged into $(1, 4, 1)$, and $(1, 1, 4)$. Likewise, $(3, 2, 1)$ can be rearranged into $(3, 1, 2)$, $(2, 1, 3)$, $(2, 3, 1)$, $(1, 2, 3)$ and $(1, 3, 2)$. Lastly, $(2, 2, 2)$ can not be rearranged into other distinct triple.

Third, in order to solve $x + y + z = 9$, we assume $x \geq y \geq z$. Then,

$$x + y + z = 9$$
$$6 + 2 + 1 = 9$$
$$5 + 3 + 1 = 9$$
$$5 + 2 + 2 = 9$$
$$4 + 4 + 1 = 9$$
$$4 + 3 + 2 = 9$$
$$3 + 3 + 3 = 9$$

Here, $(6, 2, 1)$ can be rearranged into $(6, 1, 2)$, $(1, 2, 6)$, $(1, 6, 2)$, $(2, 1, 6)$ and $(2, 6, 1)$. Likewise, $(5, 3, 1)$ can be rearranged into $(5, 1, 3)$, $(1, 3, 5)$, $(1, 5, 3)$, $(3, 1, 5)$ and $(3, 5, 1)$. Third, $(5, 2, 2)$ can be rearranged into $(2, 5, 2)$ and $(2, 2, 5)$. Fourth, $(4, 4, 1)$ can be rearranged into $(4, 1, 4)$ and $(1, 4, 4)$. Fifth, $(4, 3, 2)$ can be rearranged into $(4, 2, 3)$, $(2, 3, 4)$, $(2, 4, 3)$, $(3, 2, 4)$ and $(3, 4, 2)$. Last, $(3, 3, 3)$ cannot be rearranged into new triple.

Hence, there are $36(= 1 + 3 + 6 + 1 + 6 + 6 + 3 + 3 + 6 + 1)$ distinct triples satisfying the given condition.

24. (B) 280

There are 100 numbers with 1 as hundreds digit. Likewise, there are 100 numbers with 1 as tens digit. There are 100 numbers with 1 as units digit. Adding all together, we get 300 appearances of 1 in these numbers. If worried about the overcounts, we allow overcounts in this case. For instance, 111 has appeared in three lists, but 111 must be counted three times. Now, there are 20 numbers that should not be counted since the hundreds digit cannot be 0. Therefore, we get $280(= 300 - 20)$ number of 1s appearing in three-digit positive integers.

 # Guidance for Studying Competition Math

Studying for competition math can often be an intimidating journey, leaving many feeling uncertain about where to begin or how to proceed. This uncertainty can stem from the complexity of the material, the vast array of topics covered, and the pressure to perform well in competitive settings. It's entirely normal to experience doubts and questions along the way.

However, amidst this uncertainty, one thing remains steadfast: the power of consistency and persistence. While there may not be a straightforward or easy route to mastering competition math, committing to a consistent study routine and persistently tackling challenging problems can yield significant results over time.

Consistency in study habits, such as setting aside dedicated time each day or week to engage with math concepts, builds a strong foundation of understanding and familiarity with the material. This regular practice not only reinforces key concepts but also helps to develop problem-solving skills and strategies essential for success in competitions.

Moreover, persistence plays a crucial role in overcoming obstacles and pushing through moments of difficulty or frustration. It's natural to encounter problems that seem insurmountable or concepts that feel elusive, but persistently working through these challenges, seeking help when needed, and not giving up in the face of setbacks can lead to breakthroughs and deeper understanding.

By emphasizing the importance of consistency and persistence, aspiring mathematicians can find reassurance and support in knowing that progress is achievable through dedicated effort and determination. Each step taken, no matter how small, brings them closer to their goals and eventual success in competition math.

" The harder you work for something, the greater you'll feel when you achieve it. "

4

4.1 Problem Set

Problem 25.

Keywords: One-to-one Correspondence, Complementary Counting

Given a sequence $\{2, 3, 5, 6, 7, 10, 11, \cdots\}$, if a sequence does not contain perfect square or perfect cubes, determine the 40th term in the sequence.

(A) 46

(B) 47

(C) 48

(D) 49

(E) 50

Problem 26.

Keywords: Partition of Sets, Committee Selection

In how many ways can six people form three committees with two members each?

(A) 9

(B) 12

(C) 15

(D) 18

(E) 21

Problem 27.

Keywords: Partition of Sets, Committee Selection

In how many ways can eight people form two committees with three members and one committee with two members?

(A) 256

(B) 280

(C) 296

(D) 321

(E) 484

Problem 28.

Keywords: Card Selection, Meaning of "unordered" selection

Given a standard deck of 52 cards, in how many ways can a four-card selection contain all different cards of same suits? (Assume that the order of selection does not count.)

(A) 2120

(B) 2250

(C) 2690

(D) 2860

(E) 2980

Problem 29.

Keywords: Card Selection, Meaning of "unordered" selection

Given a standard deck of 52 cards, in how many ways can a four-card selection contain all different cards of all different suits and numbers? (Assume that the order of selection does not count.)

(A) 10000

(B) 10245

(C) 14400

(D) 17160

(E) 28651

Problem 30.

Keywords: Number of Divisors, Perfect Powers

How many natural numbers ranging from 1 to 100, inclusive, have an odd number of positive divisors?

(A) 10

(B) 11

(C) 12

(D) 13

(E) 14

Problem 31.

Keywords: Complementary Counting, Casework

Given a three-digit positive integers, count the number of integers that contain at least one 2.

(A) 200

(B) 221

(C) 225

(D) 240

(E) 252

Problem 32.

Keywords: Casework, Partition of Natural Numbers

Given a three-digit positive integers, count the number of integers consisting of only 2s and 3s that contain at least one 2 and at least one 3.

(A) 3

(B) 4

(C) 5

(D) 6

(E) 8

Problem 33.

Keywords: Casework, Permutation allowing Repetition

Given a four-digit positive integers, count the number of integers that use only 3 or 4. (We must count 3333 or 4444 as valid counts.)

(A) 8

(B) 12

(C) 16

(D) 20

(E) 24

Problem 34.

Keywords: Casework, Indicator Method

Given a four-digit positive integers, count the number of integers that contain exactly one 2 and one 3 as their digits.

(A) 360

(B) 480

(C) 600

(D) 720

(E) 810

Problem 35.

Keywords: Casework, Combination allowing Repetition, Circles and Bars

Bob has three different-looking bags made of leather. Receiving 6 coins from his friend, he wants to put them inside three bags, carrying them back home. In how many ways can he put coins inside the bags, where each bag should contain at least one coin?

(A) 10

(B) 12

(C) 14

(D) 16

(E) 18

Problem 36.

Keywords: Casework, Permutation with Repeated Letters

Which of the following counts the number of five-digit positive integers whose digits are either 1, 2, or 3, such that there are at least one 1, one 2 and one 3 in their digits?

(A) 60

(B) 90

(C) 120

(D) 150

(E) 180

4.2 Solution Manual

25. (C) 48

First, there are 6 perfect squares less than or equal to 40, i.e., $\{1, 4, 9, 16, 25, 36\}$. Likewise, there are 2 perfect cubes less than or equal to 40, i.e., $\{8, 27\}$. In this case, 1 is not counted inside a perfect-cube set because it is redundant. Now, add 40 with 6 and 2 to get 48. Notice that there is no perfect square nor cube between 40 and 48. Hence, the answer is 48.

26. (C) 15

Let there be six people. In order to form three committees with two members each, we choose two people out of six people in $\binom{6}{2}$ number of ways. Then, we choose two people out of remaining four people in $\binom{4}{2}$ number of ways. Then, the last two people are automatically chosen. Since the committees are *unordered*, we compute the answer as

$$\frac{\binom{6}{2}\binom{4}{2}\binom{2}{2}}{3!} = 15$$

27. (B) 280

Like the previous problem, we choose three people out of eight people by $\binom{8}{3}$ number of ways. Then, we choose three people out of remaining five people by $\binom{5}{3}$ number of ways. Lastly, we choose two people out of remaining two people. Since there are two groups with the same number of people, we get rid of order between the groups as

$$\frac{\binom{8}{3}\binom{5}{3}\binom{2}{2}}{2!} = 280$$

number of ways.

28. (D) 2860

There are four suits we can choose, so choose one out of four. Then, within one suit, we choose four cards out of 13 cards. Therefore, four-card selections may be formed in $4 \times \binom{13}{4} = 2860$ number of ways.

29. (D) 17160

Since we select without order, we fix the order of suits. Choose one card out of 13 hearts. Choose one card out of 12 diamonds, according to the condition. Choose one card out of 11 spades. Finally, choose one card out of 10 clubs. Hence, there are $17160(= 13 \times 12 \times 11 \times 10)$ four-card selections satisfying the given condition.

30. (A) 10

If a natural number has an odd number of positive divisors, it must be a perfect square. Let n^2 be a perfect square. Then, we may set up an inequality $1 \leq n^2 \leq 100$ such that $1 \leq n \leq 10$. Since there are 10 perfect squares, we conclude that there are 10 natural numbers having an odd number of positive divisors each.

31. (E) 252

Let $\overline{abc}$ be a three-digit positive integer. There are $9 \times 10 \times 10$ number of $\overline{abc}$s. Since each of the digit must contain at least one 2, we may perform casework as following.

1. one 2 : there are 81 numbers in $2XX$ form. On the other hand, there are 72 numbers each in $X2X$ and $XX2$ form.

2. two 2s : there are 9 numbers each in $22X$ and $2X2$ form. On the other hand, there are 8 numbers in $X22$ form.

3. three 2s : there is only one number in 222 form.

Hence, there are 252 number of integers satisfying the given condition.

One may also think about another way of solving this problem : complementary counting. There are $648(= 8 \times 9 \times 9)$ number of integers that do not contain digit 2 in their expressions. Hence, there are $252(= 900 - 648)$ number of integers satisfying the given condition.

32. (D) 6

Let a and b be the number of 2s and 3s in the digit expression, respectively. Then, $a + b = 3$ where $a \geq 1$ and $b \geq 1$. Thus, $(a, b) = (2, 1)$ or $(1, 2)$.

For the first part, if $(a, b) = (2, 1)$, we get three possibilities - 223, 232, and 322. For the second part, if $(a, b) = (1, 2)$, we get three possibilities - 233, 323, and 332. Hence, there are 6 integers consisting of only 2s and 3s satisfying the given condition.

33. (C) 16

First, let a and b be the number of 3s and 4s in the digit expression, respectively. Then, $a + b = 4$ implies that there are $(a, b) = (4, 0), (3, 1), (2, 2), (1, 3)$ and $(0, 4)$.

- $(a, b) = (4, 0)$: $\{3333\}$.

- $(a, b) = (3, 1)$: $\{3334, 3343, 3433, 4333\}$.

- $(a, b) = (2, 2)$: $\{3344, 3434, 3443, 4334, 4343, 4433\}$.

- $(a, b) = (1, 3)$: $\{3444, 4344, 4434, 4443\}$.

- $(a, b) = (0, 4)$: $\{4444\}$.

There are 16 integers consisting of 3s or 4s.

On the other hand, one may use *permutation allowing repetition*. In particular, if we let $\overline{abcd}$ as a four-digit integer, then $a, b, c, d \in \{3, 4\}$ implies that there are $16(= 2 \times 2 \times 2 \times 2)$ number of integers satisfying the given condition.

34. (E) 720

Let X be a digit other than 2 or 3. According to the condition laid out in a problem, there are 12 possible cases. For simplicity, we look at six cases when 2 appears before 3. Then, we will multiply the sum by 2, for there are symmetric cases when 2 appears after 3.

1. $23XX$: there are 64 numbers in this form.

2. $2X3X$: there are 64 numbers in this form.

3. $2XX3$: there are 64 numbers in this form.

4. $X23X$: there are 56 numbers in this form.

5. $X2X3$: there are 56 numbers in this form.

6. $XX23$: there are 56 numbers in this form.

Thus, there are 360 four-digit numbers satisfying the given condition where 2 appears before 3. Since there are exactly same number of four-digit integers such that 2 appears after 3, the answer turns out 720.

35. (A) 10

Let $a + b + c = 6$ where a, b, and c are whole numbers representing the number of coins in each bag. Then, the condition stated in the problem states that $(a, b, c) = (4, 1, 1), (3, 2, 1)$ and $(2, 2, 2)$, assuming that $a \geq b \geq c$. Since the bags have their looks different, we put orders back by arranging $(4, 1, 1)$ into $(4, 1, 1)$, $(1, 4, 1)$ and $(1, 1, 4)$. Likewise, we put order to $(3, 2, 1)$ into six different triples. On the other hand, $(2, 2, 2)$ has only one triple - itself. Thus, there are 10 ways that he can put 6 coins to three bags, according to the given condition.

36. (D) 150

Let a, b, and c be the number of appearances of 1, 2, and 3, respectively, in a five-digit number. Then, $a + b + c = 5$ where $a \geq 1$, $b \geq 1$ and $c \geq 1$. According to the given condition, we write down all possibilities.

$$a + b + c = 5$$
$$3 + 1 + 1 = 5$$
$$1 + 3 + 1 = 5$$
$$1 + 1 + 3 = 5$$
$$2 + 2 + 1 = 5$$
$$2 + 1 + 2 = 5$$
$$1 + 2 + 2 = 5$$

If $(a, b, c) = (3, 1, 1)$, then we are looking at the arrangement of 11123. This number may arrange in $\dfrac{5!}{3!1!1!} = 20$ number of ways. Since $(a, b, c) = (3, 1, 1)$, $(1, 3, 1)$ and $(1, 1, 3)$ are symmetric, we simply multiply 3 to 20 to get 60 number of possibilities.

Likewise, if $(a, b, c) = (2, 2, 1)$, then we are looking at the arrangement of 11223. This number may arrange in $\dfrac{5!}{2!2!1!} = 30$ number of ways. Since $(a, b, c) = (2, 2, 1)$, $(2, 1, 2)$ and $(1, 2, 2)$ are symmetric, we multiply 3 to 30 to get 90 number of possibilities.

Thus, there are $150 (= 60 + 90)$ number of five-digit integers satisfying the given condition.

Quotes from Mathematicans

"The only way to learn mathematics is to do mathematics." - Paul Halmos

"In mathematics, the art of proposing a question must be held of higher value than solving it." - Georg Cantor

"Mathematics is not about numbers, equations, computations, or algorithms: it is about understanding." - William Paul Thurston

"It is not enough to have a good mind; the main thing is to use it well." - René Descartes

"The essence of mathematics lies in its freedom." - Georg Cantor

"In mathematics, the truth is somewhere out there in a place no one knows, beyond all the beaten paths. And it is worth seeking." - Yōko Ogawa

"Mathematics, rightly viewed, possesses not only truth but supreme beauty." - Bertrand Russell

"Mathematics is the most beautiful and most powerful creation of the human spirit." - Stefan Banach

"Mathematics is the language in which God has written the universe." - Galileo Galilei

"Every accomplishment starts with the decision to try."

5

5.1 Problem Set

Problem 37.

Keywords: Greatest Common Divisor, Complementary Counting

If a triple of positive integers (r, s, t) satisfies the following condition :
$1 \leq r, s, t \leq 3$, and the greatest common divisor of r, s, and t is 1, compute the number of distinct triples of (r, s, t).

(A) 6

(B) 15

(C) 24

(D) 25

(E) 27

Problem 38.

Keywords: Casework, Partition of Natural Numbers

In how many ways can 10 be partitioned into at most three whole numbers? Here, a whole number is a non-negative integer.

(A) 12

(B) 13

(C) 14

(D) 15

(E) 16

Problem 39.

Keywords: Casework, Partition of Natural Numbers

Using *a single straight line cut*, if a 30×25 grid paper is to be cut into two rectangular grid papers such that the side length of two rectangular grid papers is a whole number, how many different pairs of rectangular grid papers can be produced? In this pair, we consider a pair formed by 14×25 and 16×25 paper equal to the pair formed by 16×25 and 14×25 papers.

(A) 26

(B) 27

(C) 28

(D) 29

(E) 30

Problem 40.

Keywords: Combination allowing Repetition, One-to-one Correspondence

If eight identical-looking marbles are to be placed in four distinct urns, and each urn must contain at least one marble, in how many ways can it be done?

(A) 30

(B) 35

(C) 40

(D) 45

(E) 50

Problem 41.

Keywords: Combination allowing Repetition, Casework

If six identical-looking marbles are to be placed in at most four distinct urns, in how many ways can it be done?

(A) 35

(B) 36

(C) 56

(D) 84

(E) 126

Problem 42.

Keywords: Casework, Permutation allowing Repeated Letters, Partition of Natural Numbers

There are four cards, each of which can be colored either red, yellow, or green. If all colors must be used at least once, in how many different ways can all four cards be arranged in a line? (For example, $RRYG$ and $RRGY$ are considered distinct.)

(A) 30

(B) 36

(C) 42

(D) 48

(E) 54

Problem 43.

Keywords: Casework, Partition of Natural Numbers, Combination allowing Repetition, Permutation allowing Repeated Letters

There are six equally spaced six dots in a straight line. Each dot can be colored either red, yellow, or green. If all colors must be used at least twice and adjacent dots can be colored with the same color, there are N number of ways to color these dots, satisfying the given condition. Compute the value of $\frac{N}{10}$.

(A) 5

(B) 6

(C) 9

(D) 12

(E) 15

Problem 44.

Keywords: Partition of Sets, Committee Selection

If there are five freshmen who joins the secret society, in how many ways can they be teamed up into three groups such that each group has at least one member?

(A) 15

(B) 20

(C) 25

(D) 30

(E) 35

Problem 45.

Keywords: Partition of Sets, Committee Selection

A platoon of ten soldiers are ready to execute the operation such that two squads of soldiers must jointly move at the same time. Assuming that each squad consists of at least two soldiers as battle buddies, in how many ways can they form two *unordered* squads?

(A) 501

(B) 504

(C) 509

(D) 1001

(E) 1002

Problem 46.

Keywords: Digits, Complementary Counting, Permutation with Restriction

How many four-digit positive integers can be formed such that the sum of middle two digits exceeds 10?

(A) 135

(B) 270

(C) 810

(D) 1620

(E) 3240

Problem 47.

Keywords: One-to-one Function, Permutation with Restriction

Let $X = \{1, 2, 3, 4, 5, 6\}$. Determine the number of $f : X \longrightarrow X$, where it is one-to-one function, $f(\text{even}) = \text{odd}$, and $f(\text{odd}) = \text{even}$.

(A) 4

(B) 9

(C) 25

(D) 36

(E) 49

Problem 48.

Keywords: One-to-one Function, Combination

Let $X = \{1, 2, 3, 4, 5, 6\}$. Determine the number of $f : X \longrightarrow X$, satisfying the following conditions.

- For all $a, b \in X$, if $1 \leq a < b \leq 3$, then $f(a) > f(b)$.

- $|f(X)| = |X|$, i.e., f is one-to-one.

(A) 100

(B) 120

(C) 140

(D) 160

(E) 180

5.2 Solution Manual

37. (D) 25

If there are three 1s, then $(r, s, t) = (1, 1, 1)$. If there are two 1s, then $(r, s, t) = (1, 1, 2)$ or $(1, 1, 3)$. In this case, $(1, 1, 2)$, $(1, 2, 1)$ and $(2, 1, 1)$ are distinct triples made out of $(1, 1, 2)$. Likewise, $(1, 1, 3)$, $(1, 3, 1)$, $(3, 1, 1)$ are distinct triples made out of $(1, 1, 3)$.

On the other hand, if there is only one 1, then (r, s, t) can be written as $(1, 2, 3)$, $(1, 2, 2)$ and $(1, 3, 3)$. The first sub-case produces 6 possible arrangements. The second and third sub-cases produce 3 possible arrangements.

If there is no 1, then (r, s, t) must be rearrangements of $(2, 2, 3)$ or $(2, 3, 3)$, each of which produces 3 different arrangements. Hence, the total number of (r, s, t) satisfying the given condition is 25.

38. (C) 14

Without loss of generality, assume that $a \geq b \geq c \geq 0$. Then,

$$a + b + c = 10$$
$$10 + 0 + 0 = 10$$
$$9 + 1 + 0 = 10$$
$$8 + 2 + 0 = 10$$
$$7 + 3 + 0 = 10$$
$$6 + 4 + 0 = 10$$
$$5 + 5 + 0 = 10$$
$$8 + 1 + 1 = 10$$
$$7 + 2 + 1 = 10$$
$$6 + 3 + 1 = 10$$
$$5 + 4 + 1 = 10$$
$$6 + 2 + 2 = 10$$
$$5 + 3 + 2 = 10$$
$$4 + 4 + 2 = 10$$
$$4 + 3 + 3 = 10$$

There are 14 partitions of 10 into at most 3 whole numbers.

39. (B) 27

Let $a + b = 30$ for $a \geq b \geq 1$. Then, $(a, b) = (29, 1), (28, 2), \cdots, (15, 15)$. There are 15 pairs of (a, b). Likewise, let $c + d = 25$ for $c \geq d \geq 1$. Then, $(c, d) = (24, 1), (23, 2), \cdots, (13, 12)$. There are 12 pairs of (c, d). Thus, $15 + 12 = 27$ possible distinct cuts.

40. (B) 35

Let a, b, c, and d be the number of marbles placed in urns, respectively. Then, $a + b + c + d = 8$ where $a, b, c, d \geq 1$. In order to use 1-to-1 correspondence, we set $a = a' + 1$, $b = b' + 1$, $c = c' + 1$, and $d = d' + 1$.

Thus, $a + b + c + d = 8$ implies that $a' + b' + c' + d' = 4$. Using circles and bars, we conclude that eight marbles can be placed in four distinct urns in $\binom{7}{3} = 35$ ways.

41. (D) 84

Let x, y, z, and w be the number of marbles placed in urns, respectively. Then, $x + y + z + w = 6$ where x, y, z, and w are whole numbers.

Then, using the circles and bars, we may conclude that six marbles can be placed in four different urns in $\binom{9}{3} = 84$ ways.

42. (B) 36

Let r, y and g be the number of cards with red, yellow and green colors, respectively. Then, $r + y + g = 4$ where $r, y, g \geq 1$ implies that $(r, y, g) = (2, 1, 1)$, $(1, 2, 1)$ and $(1, 1, 2)$. For $(r, y, g) = (2, 1, 1)$, arranging these cards into a line results in 12 different arrangements, i.e., $RRYG$, $RRGY$, $RGRY$, $RYRG$, $RYGR$, $RGYR$, $GRRY$, $YRRG$, $YRGR$, $GRYR$, $GYRR$, and $YGRR$.

Likewise, we get 12 different arrangements for $(r, y, g) = (1, 2, 1)$ and $(1, 1, 2)$. Thus, there are 36 different ways to arrange four cards satisfying the given condition.

43. (C) 9

If all colors must be used at least twice, then the only possible triple $(r, y, g) = (2, 2, 2)$. Thus, $N = \binom{6}{2, 2, 2} = \dfrac{6!}{2!2!2!} = 90$. Hence, $\dfrac{N}{10} = 9$.

44. (A) 25

Without loss of generality, assume $a \geq b \geq c \geq 1$. Then, $a + b + c = 5$ implies that $(a, b, c) = (3, 1, 1)$ and $(2, 2, 1)$. This indicates that there are

$$\frac{\binom{5}{3}\binom{2}{1}\binom{1}{1}}{2!} + \frac{\binom{5}{2}\binom{3}{2}\binom{1}{1}}{2!} = 25$$

number of arrangements of people into three groups.

45. (A) 501

Let a and b be the number of soldiers in the first and second squad, respectively. Then, $a + b = 10$ for $a, b \geq 2$. We only care about forming two squads, so we partition 10 soldiers into two groups. Without loss of generality, assume $a \geq b$. Then, $(a, b) = (8, 2), (7, 3), (6, 4)$ and $(5, 5)$. Hence, there are 501 ways to partition 10 soldiers into two groups, i.e., the sum of

$$\binom{10}{8}\binom{2}{2} + \binom{10}{7}\binom{3}{3} + \binom{10}{6}\binom{4}{4} + \frac{1}{2!}\binom{10}{5}\binom{5}{5} = 501.$$

46. (D) 3240

Let $\overline{abcd}$ be a four-digit positive integer. Then, $b + c > 10$. Thus, we find $(b, c) = (9, 9), (9, 8), (8, 9), (9, 7), (8, 8), (7, 9), \cdots (9, 2), (8, 3), \cdots, (2, 9)$. In fact, there are $\dfrac{8 \cdot 9}{2} = 36$ number of pairs for b and c. Now, $1 \leq a \leq 9$ and $0 \leq d \leq 9$ imply that $36 \cdot 9 \cdot 10 = 3240$ $\overline{abcd}$s satisfy the given condition.

47. (D) 36

Since $f(\{2, 4, 6\}) = \{1, 3, 5\}$ and $f(\{1, 3, 5\}) = \{2, 4, 6\}$, we have to decide what $f(2)$, $f(4)$ and $f(6)$ are, and $f(1)$, $f(3)$, and $f(5)$ are.

There are $3!$ number of ways to decide $f(2)$, $f(4)$, and $f(6)$. Likewise, there are $3!$ number of ways to decide $f(1)$, $f(3)$, and $f(5)$. Hence, there are $36(= 3! \times 3!)$ number of $f : X \longrightarrow X$ satisfying the given condition.

48. (B) 120

The first condition already states that $f(1) \neq f(2) \neq f(3)$. Since $f(1) > f(2) > f(3)$, there are $\binom{6}{3}$ number of three values we may choose for $f(1)$, $f(2)$, and $f(3)$. For $f(4)$, $f(5)$, and $f(6)$, there are three other unselected values, so there are $3!$ number of ways to assign three remaining y-values to $f(4)$, $f(5)$, and $f(6)$. Hence, the answer must be $\binom{6}{3} \times 3! = 120$.

Designed and Tailored for
Your Successful Journey on Competition Math

"Believe in yourself, and all that you are capable of achieving."

6

6.1 Problem Set

Problem 49.

Keywords: Triangular Numbers, Combination

A tennis league involves 12 players, each of whom plays 2 games with each of the other players. How many games were played in total?

(A) 48

(B) 54

(C) 66

(D) 132

(E) 148

Problem 50.

Keywords: Combination allowing Repetition, Circles and Bars, Stars and Bars

How many integers from 0 to 9999 have their sum of digits equal 9?

(A) 66

(B) 120

(C) 180

(D) 220

(E) 242

Problem 51.

Keywords: Principle of Multiplication in Counting, Permutation allowing Repetition

If each of the four students who just came out of the university library must choose one restaurant out of five different ones, in how many ways can they choose the restaurants to go and eat?

(A) 120

(B) 625

(C) 1000

(D) 1024

(E) 2048

Problem 52.

Keywords: Partition of Sets, Committee Selection

If a group of five people must join three different clubs, where there is no club with no member, in how many ways can they join the clubs if there are only two clubs with the same number of members?

(A) 60

(B) 90

(C) 120

(D) 150

(E) 180

Problem 53.

Keywords: One-to-one Correspondence, Hockey-Stick Identity, Indicator Method

Find the number of non-negative integer triples (x, y, z) such that $x + y + z \leq 5$.

(A) 52

(B) 56

(C) 60

(D) 64

(E) 66

Problem 54.

Keywords: Principle of Multiplication in Probability

There are seven people, including Janice and Denice, arranged in a line in front of ticket boxes at movie theater. The probability that Janice and Denice are apart from one another can be written as $\frac{m}{n}$ where m and n are relatively prime positive integers. Determine $m + n$.

(A) 9

(B) 10

(C) 11

(D) 12

(E) 13

Problem 55.

Keywords: Principle of Multiplication in Probability, Circular Probability

There are five people, including Annie and Amy, to be seated around a circular table. The probability that Annie and Amy are next to each other can be written as $\frac{m}{n}$ where m and n are relatively prime positive integers. Determine $m + n$.

(A) 3

(B) 5

(C) 10

(D) 12

(E) 15

Problem 56.

Keywords: Symmetric Count, Complementary Probability

If David rolls three fair six-sided dice, the probability that he rolls more evens than odds can be written as $\frac{m}{n}$ where m and n are relatively prime positive integers. Determine $m + n$.

(A) 3

(B) 7

(C) 10

(D) 12

(E) 18

Problem 57.

Keywords: Symmetric Count, Complementary Probability

If David rolls six fair six-sided dice, the probability that he rolls more evens than odds can be written as $\frac{m}{n}$ where m and n are relatively prime positive integers. Determine $m + n$.

(A) 39

(B) 41

(C) 43

(D) 45

(E) 47

Problem 58.

Keywords: Principle of Multiplication in Probability, Circular Probability

If 8 people including Alice and Alex are seated at random around a circular table, the probability that Alice and Alex are seated next to each other can be written as $\dfrac{m}{n}$ where m and n are relatively prime positive integers. Determine $m+n$.

(A) 7

(B) 9

(C) 11

(D) 13

(E) 15

Problem 59.

Keywords: Geometric Probability, Hypotenuse = Circumdiameter

A point P is randomly chosen inside $ABCD$. A diagram below shows one example of selecting P inside $ABCD$. The probability that APB is *obtuse* can be written as $\dfrac{\pi}{N}$ where N is a positive integer. Determine the exact value of N.

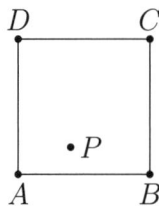

(A) 6   (B) 8   (C) 10   (D) 12   (E) 14

Problem 60.

Keywords: Complementary Probability

Three standard dice are rolled. The probability that the product of three numbers on the top faces exceeds 4 can be written as $\dfrac{m}{n}$ where m and n are relatively prime positive integers. Determine $m+n$.

(A) 411

(B) 413

(C) 415

(D) 417

(E) 419

6.2 Solution Manual

49. (D) 132

This is a constructive counting. Choose two tennis players out of twelve players in $\binom{12}{2} = 66$ number of ways. Then, each pair plays twice, so multiply it by 2 to get 132.

50. (D) 220

This is a classic question of circles and bars. Let $\overline{abcd}$ be an integer between 0 and 9999, inclusive. Then, $a + b + c + d = 9$, where a, b, c, and d are allowed to be 0.

Hence, circles and bars indicate that there are three bars and nine circles to be arranged. Therefore, there are $\binom{12}{3} = \frac{12!}{3!9!} = 220$ integers ranging from 0 to 9999 such that the sum of digits equals 9.

51. (B) 625

This is a typical question about permutation allowing repetition. The first student has five restaurants to choose. The second student also has five ones to choose. This continues upto the last student.

Hence, $5^4 = 625$ is the number of ways that four students can choose one restaurant out of five restaurants, allowing repeated choices.

52. (D) 150

Let a, b, and c be the number of members in three clubs.

$$a + b + c = 3 + 1 + 1$$
$$= 2 + 2 + 1$$

Hence, $\frac{1}{2!}\binom{5}{3}\binom{2}{1}\binom{1}{1} + \frac{1}{2!}\binom{5}{2}\binom{3}{2}\binom{1}{1} = 25$. So, we multiply 25 by $3!$ to distribute these groups into three clubs.

53. (B) 56

This is a hockey-stick identity. $x + y + z = 5$ has $\binom{7}{2}$ number of triples.

$x + y + z = 4$ has $\binom{6}{2}$ number of triples. $x + y + z = 3$ has $\binom{5}{2}$ number of triples.

$x + y + z = 2$ has $\binom{4}{2}$ number of triples. $x + y + z = 1$ has $\binom{3}{2}$ number of triples.

Lastly, $x + y + z = 0$ has $\binom{2}{2}$ number of triples. According to hockey-stick identity,

$$\binom{7}{2} + \binom{6}{2} + \binom{5}{2} + \binom{4}{2} + \binom{3}{2} + \binom{2}{2} = \binom{8}{3} = 56.$$

54. **(D)** 12

$$①②③④⑤⑥⑦$$

If Janice stands at ① or ⑦, the probability for Denice to stand becomes $\frac{5}{6}$. On the other hand, if Janice stands somewhere else, then the probability for Denice to stand turns into $\frac{4}{6}$. Hence,

$$\frac{1}{7} \times \frac{5}{6} + \frac{5}{7} \times \frac{4}{6} + \frac{1}{7} \times \frac{5}{6} = \frac{5}{7}$$

Thus, $m + n = 5 + 7 = 12$.

55. **(A)** 3
If Annie sits anywhere with the probability of $\frac{5}{5}$, Amy may sit next to Annie with the probability of $\frac{2}{4}$. Hence, $\frac{5}{5} \times \frac{2}{4} = \frac{1}{2}$. Thus, $m + n = 1 + 2 = 3$.

56. **(A)** 3
The probability of having more evens than odds equals that of having more odds than evens because there can't be the same number of odds and evens since David is rolling odd times. Thus, the probability must be $\frac{1}{2}$. Therefore, $m + n = 1 + 2 = 3$.

57. **(C)** 43
Let q be the probability of having the same number of evens and odds. Let p be the probability of having more evens than odds, or vice versa. Since q can be computed as

$$\binom{6}{3} \left(\frac{1}{2} \right)^6 = \frac{5}{16},$$

we conclude that $2p = \frac{11}{16}$. Hence, $p = \frac{11}{32}$. The sum of 11 and 32 equals 43.

58. **(B)** 9
Let Alice be seated with the probability of $\frac{8}{8}$. Then, the probability that Alex can sit next to Alice can be written as $\frac{2}{7}$. Therefore, the probability that Alice and Alex are seated next to each other is $\frac{8}{8} \times \frac{2}{7} = \frac{2}{7}$. Thus, $m + n = 2 + 7 = 9$.

59. (B) 8

Look at the following figure.

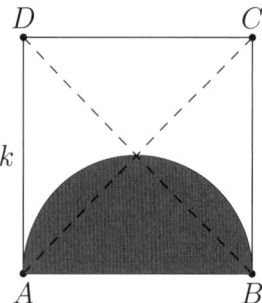

As shown in the diagram above, let k be the length of a square. Then, the area of the square equals k^2. Similarly, the area of the shaded semicircle can be written as $\dfrac{k^2\pi}{8}$. Hence, the probability that S is selected inside the shaded region equals $\dfrac{k^2\pi/8}{k^2} = \dfrac{\pi}{8}$. This implies that $N = 8$.

60. (E) 419

Let a, b, and c be the values on top faces of each die, respectively. Then, there are $216(= 6^3)$ number of ways to choose a, b and c. The number of triples satisfying $abc > 4$ seems large enough, so we choose to count when $abc \leq 4$.

1. $abc = 4 : (a, b, c) = (4, 1, 1)$, $(1, 4, 1)$, $(1, 1, 4)$, $(2, 2, 1)$, $(2, 1, 2)$, and $(1, 2, 2)$.

2. $abc = 3 : (a, b, c) = (3, 1, 1)$, $(1, 3, 1)$, and $(1, 1, 3)$.

3. $abc = 2 : (a, b, c) = (2, 1, 1)$, $(1, 2, 1)$, and $(1, 1, 2)$.

4. $abc = 1 : (a, b, c) = (1, 1, 1)$

In other words, there are 13 triples that do not satisfy the given condition. Hence, there are 203 number of triples satisfying the original condition. Thus, the probability we want must be $\dfrac{203}{216}$, so the answer is $203 + 216 = 419$.

"Turn your setbacks into comebacks and your doubts into confidence."

7

7.1 Problem Set

Problem 61.

Keywords: Principle of Multiplication in Probability

If 10 people including Somi and Sandy are seated in a row, the probability that Somi is at one end and Sandy is at the other end can be written as $\dfrac{m}{n}$ where m and n are relatively prime positive integers. Determine $m + n$.

(A) 44

(B) 45

(C) 46

(D) 47

(E) 48

Problem 62.

Keywords: Principle of Multiplication in Probability, Circular Probability, Indicator Method

If 6 people including Tom and Tim are randomly arranged in a circle, the probability that Tom and Tim are not adjacent can be written as $\dfrac{m}{n}$ where m and n are relatively prime positive integers. Determine $m + n$.

(A) 5

(B) 6

(C) 7

(D) 8

(E) 9

Problem 63.

Keywords: Principle of Multiplication in Probability, Indicator Method

If 12 people including Max and Mia are standing in a line, the probability that Max and Mia are standing next to each other but not at the ends of the line can be written as $\dfrac{m}{n}$ where m and n are relatively prime positive integers. Determine $m + n$.

(A) 25

(B) 27

(C) 29

(D) 31

(E) 33

Problem 64.

Keywords: Principle of Multiplication in Probability, Circular Probability

If 10 people including Lily and Leo are seated at random around a circular table, the probability that Lily and Leo are seated opposite each other can be written as $\frac{m}{n}$ where m and n are relatively prime positive integers. Determine $m + n$.

(A) 9

(B) 10

(C) 11

(D) 12

(E) 13

Problem 65.

Keywords: Getting Rid of Orders, Probability with Restriction

If 7 people including John, Jane, and Jill are standing in a line, the probability that John is ahead of Jane and Jill can be written as $\frac{m}{n}$ where m and n are relatively prime positive integers. Determine $m + n$.

(A) 4

(B) 10

(C) 16

(D) 20

(E) 24

Problem 66.

Keywords: Principle of Multiplication in Probability, Circular Probability

If 11 people including Kay and Kyle are seated at random around a circular table, the probability that Kay and Kyle are not next to each other can be written as $\frac{m}{n}$ where m and n are relatively prime positive integers. Determine $m + n$.

(A) 6

(B) 7

(C) 8

(D) 9

(E) 10

Problem 67.

Keywords: Principle of Multiplication in Probability, Circular Probability

If 5 people including Pat and Pam are randomly arranged in a circle, the probability that Pam occupies Pat's closest right seat, assuming that Pat sits towards the circle, can be written as $\frac{m}{n}$ where m and n are relatively prime positive integers. Determine $m + n$.

(A) 4

(B) 5

(C) 9

(D) 14

(E) 23

Problem 68.

Keywords: Principle of Multiplication in Probability, Indicator Method

If 13 people including Mike and Mandy are standing in a line, the probability that Mike and Mandy are not next to each other and not at the ends of the line can be written as $\frac{m}{n}$ where m and n are relatively prime positive integers. Determine $m + n$.

(A) 37

(B) 39

(C) 41

(D) 43

(E) 45

Problem 69.

Keywords: Principle of Multiplication in Probability, Indicator Method

If 8 people including Fred and George are seated at random around a circular table, the probability that Fred and George are seated next to each other or opposite each other can be written as $\frac{m}{n}$ where m and n are relatively prime positive integers. Determine $m + n$.

(A) 9

(B) 10

(C) 11

(D) 12

(E) 13

Problem 70.

Keywords: Constructive Probability, Casework, Counting vs. Probability

If all integers in $\{1, 2, 3, 4, 5, 6\}$ are placed in the vertices of regular hexagon, the probability that the sum of any consecutive pair of integers is odd can be written as $\frac{m}{n}$ where m and n are relatively prime positive integers. Determine $m + n$.

(A) 10

(B) 11

(C) 12

(D) 13

(E) 14

Problem 71.

Keywords: Probability with Distinct Kinds, Order Locked or Not

A pair of dice is rolled until the sum of the two numbers is 9. The probability that the sum 9 is obtained at the 3rd toss, but not before, can be written as $\frac{m}{n}$ where m and n are relatively prime positive integers. Find $m + n$.

(A) 789

(B) 791

(C) 793

(D) 795

(E) 797

Problem 72.

Keywords: Geometric Probability

Amy and Victoria each arrive at a bus terminal between $12:00$ and $1:00$. Each stays at a terminal for 10 minutes. The probability that they meet at the terminal is $\frac{m}{n}$ where m and n are relatively prime positive integers. Determine the sum of m and n.

(A) 41

(B) 43

(C) 45

(D) 47

(E) 49

7.2 Solution Manual

61. (C) 46

$$①②③④⑤⑥⑦⑧⑨$$

If Somi seats at either ① or ⑨, Sandy must sit in the remaining seat. Hence, the probability that we should compute can be written as $\frac{2}{10} \times \frac{1}{9} = \frac{1}{45}$. Thus $m + n = 1 + 45 = 46$.

62. (D) 8

Let Tom be seated with the probability of $\frac{6}{6}$. Then, the probability that Tim can be seated is $\frac{3}{5}$. Thus, the probability we want is $\frac{6}{6} \times \frac{3}{5} = \frac{3}{5}$. Thus, $m + m = 3 + 5 = 8$.

63. (A) 25

$$①②③④⑤⑥⑦⑧⑨⑩⑪⑫$$

If Mike sits at ② or ⑪, Mia can sit at one seat, respectively. Otherwise, Mia can sit in two possible seats. Hence,

$$\frac{1}{12} \times \frac{1}{11} + \frac{8}{12} \times \frac{2}{11} + \frac{1}{12} \times \frac{1}{11} = \frac{18}{132} = \frac{3}{22}$$

Thus, $m + n = 3 + 22 = 25$.

64. (B) 10

Let Lily be seated with the probability of $\frac{10}{10}$. Then, Leo can sit at one seat with the probability of $\frac{1}{9}$. Thus, $\frac{10}{10} \times \frac{1}{9} = \frac{1}{9}$. Therefore, $m + n = 1 + 9 = 10$.

65. (A) 4

Get rid of orders between John, Jane, and Jill by $\frac{7!}{3!}$. However, since Jane and Jill can switch orders, we multiply the given number by 2!. Thus, the probability we want to compute is

$$\frac{\frac{7!}{3!} \times 2!}{7!} = \frac{1}{3}$$

Thus, $m + n = 1 + 3 = 4$.

66. (D) 9

We use complementary probability. Let p be the probability that Kay and Kyle sit next to each other. Then, $p = \dfrac{11}{11} \times \dfrac{2}{10} = \dfrac{1}{5}$. Therefore, $1 - \dfrac{1}{5} = \dfrac{4}{5}$. Thus, $m + n = 4 + 5 = 9$.

67. (B) 5

Let Pat be seated with the probability of $\dfrac{5}{5}$. Then, Pam can be seated with the probability of $\dfrac{1}{4}$. Thus, $\dfrac{5}{5} \times \dfrac{1}{4} = \dfrac{1}{4}$. In conclusion, $m + n = 1 + 4 = 5$.

68. (C) 41

$$①②③④⑤⑥⑦⑧⑨⑩⑪⑫⑬$$

If Mike sits at ② or ⑫, Mandy can sit at nine seats, respectively. Otherwise, Mia can sit in eight possible seats. Hence,

$$\frac{1}{13} \times \frac{9}{12} + \frac{9}{13} \times \frac{8}{12} + \frac{1}{13} \times \frac{9}{12} = \frac{90}{156} = \frac{15}{26}$$

Thus, $m + n = 15 + 26 = 41$.

69. (B) 10

Let Fred be seated at any seat with the probability of $\dfrac{8}{8}$. Then, George can sit satisfying the given condition with the probability of $\dfrac{3}{7}$. Hence, $\dfrac{8}{8} \times \dfrac{3}{7} = \dfrac{3}{7}$. Thus, $m + n = 3 + 7 = 10$.

70. (B) 11

Either we place even, odd, even, odd, even, odd, in that order, or odd, even, odd, even, odd, even, in this order. Hence, there are $3! \times 3! \times 2! = 72$ ways to arrange the numbers in six spots. Thus, $\dfrac{72}{6!} = \dfrac{72}{720} = \dfrac{1}{10}$. Therefore, $m + n = 1 + 10 = 11$.

71. (C) 793

Let p be the probability of having the sum of two numbers as 9. Out of 36 pairs, there are 4 pairs resulting in the sum of 9. This implies that $p = \dfrac{1}{9}$.

Since the first two roll must be unsuccessful, the probability that the sum 9 is obtained at the 3rd toss, but not before, is $\dfrac{8}{9} \times \dfrac{8}{9} \times \dfrac{1}{9} = \dfrac{64}{729}$. Thus, the answer is 793.

72. **(D)** 47

Look at the following figure, where A stands for Amy's time, and V stands for Victoria's time.

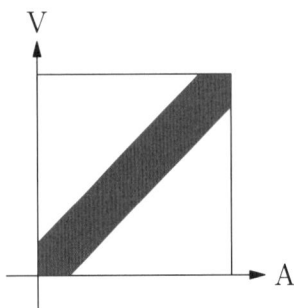

The hexagon can easily be found by getting rid of two right triangles out of a square. Since the square has the size of 60×60, we take out 50×50 from it, so that the remaining figure has the area of 1100. Thus, the probability that they meet up with one another equals $\frac{1100}{3600} = \frac{11}{36}$. The answer must be 47.

Designed and Tailored for
Your Successful Journey on Competition Math

" The pain of studying is temporary, but the pride of achieving is forever."

8

8.1   Problem Set

Problem 73.

Keywords: Geometric Probability, Conditional Probability, Independent/Dependent Events

If two points are chosen at random on a circle, then the probability that the chord length between the two points is at least the length of its radius is $\frac{m}{n}$ where m and n are relatively prime. Compute $m + n$.

(A) 5

(B) 7

(C) 9

(D) 11

(E) 13

Problem 74.

Keywords: Expected Value

Bo rolls a fair six-sided die until he gets a prime number. What is the expected number of times he rolls a die? (You may assume that the expected value in this problem is the reciprocal of a probability.)

(A) 1

(B) 2

(C) 3

(D) 4

(E) 5

Problem 75.

Keywords: Recurrence Relation, Non-adjacency

In how many ways can a string of 0s and 1s of length 5 can be made if there cannot be two consecutive 0s nor 1s? For example, 10101 is accepted as a proper string, but 11001 is not.

(A) 2

(B) 4

(C) 8

(D) 16

(E) 32

Problem 76.

Keywords: Simon's Favorite Factoring Technique

Compute the number of positive integer pairs (x, y) satisfying $\frac{1}{x} + \frac{1}{y} = \frac{1}{4}$.

(A) 2

(B) 3

(C) 4

(D) 5

(E) 6

Problem 77.

Keywords: One-to-one Correspondence, Hockey-Stick Identity

Determine the number of non-negative odd integer triples (x, y, z) such that $x + y + z \leq 15$.

(A) 9

(B) 36

(C) 84

(D) 126

(E) 144

Problem 78.

Keywords: Complementary Probability

If three-digit string using 6 digits, $\{1, 2, 3, 4, 5, 6\}$, is formed, allowing repeated digits, the probability that at least one 3 is included can be written as $\frac{m}{n}$ where m and n are relatively prime positive integers. Determine $m + n$.

(A) 299

(B) 301

(C) 303

(D) 305

(E) 307

Problem 79.

Keywords: Difference of Squares, Parity

Compute the number of positive integer pairs (a, b) such that $a^2 - b^2 = 24$.

(A) 1

(B) 2

(C) 3

(D) 4

(E) 5

Problem 80.

Keywords: Permutation allowing Repetition, Complementary Counting

Given a set of integers $\{a, b, c, d, e\}$, the number of triples (A, B, C) such that $\emptyset \neq A \subset B \subset C = \{a, b, c, d, e\}$ equals n. Determine the value of n.

(A) 32

(B) 200

(C) 211

(D) 225

(E) 243

Problem 81.

Keywords: Divisors, Principle of Inclusion and Exclusion

The probability that a positive integer divisor of $2^2 3^2 5^2 7^2$ is a multiple of 2 or 3 can be written as $\dfrac{m}{n}$ where m and n are relatively prime positive integers. Determine $m + n$.

(A) 15

(B) 17

(C) 19

(D) 21

(E) 23

Problem 82.

Keywords: Constructive Probability

If eight students - four freshmen, two sophomores, and two juniors - are grouped together into three committees of three members, three members, and two members each, the probability that juniors are in the same group can be written as $\frac{m}{n}$ where m and n are relatively prime positive integers. Determine $m + n$.

(A) 5

(B) 20

(C) 37

(D) 67

(E) 71

Problem 83.

Keywords: Labeling, Digits

Given a two-digit positive integers $\overline{ab}$, reversing its digits is greater than the original number by 18. Find the total number of such $\overline{ab}$s.

(A) 4

(B) 5

(C) 6

(D) 7

(E) 8

Problem 84.

Keywords: Divisibility, Casework, Combination allowing Repetition

If a three-digit positive integer is divisible by 9, where none of the digits is 1, compute the total number of such three-digit integers.

(A) 70

(B) 72

(C) 74

(D) 76

(E) 81

8.2 Solution Manual

73. (A) 5

Choose a point at a circle with the probability of $\dfrac{2\pi r}{2\pi r} = 1$. Then, the second point can be chosen with the probability of $\dfrac{240°}{360°} = \dfrac{2}{3}$. Since the angle formed by the first point and the second point must be greater than $60°$ or smaller than $-60°$ where the angle must be chosen from $-360°$ and $360°$.

74. (B) 2

Let E be the expected value. Then,

$$E = \frac{1}{2}(1) + \frac{1}{2}(1 + E)$$

Hence, $E = 2$.

75. (A) 2

It is easy to count them directly, i.e., $\{10101, 01010\}$.

76. (D) 5

This is a typical application of simon's factoring technique and parities. Since $\dfrac{1}{x} + \dfrac{1}{y} = \dfrac{1}{4}$ can be written as $4x + 4y = xy$, we get $xy - 4x - 4y = 0$. Hence, $xy - 4x - 4y + 16 = (x - 4)(y - 4) = 16$. Therefore, there are 5 pairs of (x, y) satisfying the equation.

77. (C) 84

Let $x = 2a + 1$ for $a \geq 0$, $y = 2b + 1$ for $y \geq 0$, and $z = 2c + 1$ for $z \geq 0$. Then, $2a + 1 + 2b + 1 + 2c + 1 \leq 15$ implies $2a + 2b + 2c \leq 12$. Hence, $a + b + c \leq 6$. Using the 1-to-1 correspondence, let $a + b + c + d = 6$ for $d \geq 0$.

There are $\dbinom{9}{3}$ number of triples (a, b, c) satisfying the given inequality, using circles and bars. The answer is 84.

78. (E) 307

Complementary probability can be computed as $1 - \dfrac{5^3}{6^3} = 1 - \dfrac{125}{216} = \dfrac{91}{216}$. Hence, $m + n = 91 + 216 = 307$.

79. (B) 2

$$a^2 - b^2 = 24$$
$$(a - b)(a + b) = 24$$
$$2 \cdot 12 = 24$$
$$4 \cdot 6 = 24$$

There are two pairs (a, b) satisfying the given equation $a^2 - b^2 = 24$.

80. (C) 211

Let $C = \{a, b, c, d, e\}$. Then, sets A, B, and C make A, $B \setminus A$ and $C \setminus B$. Hence, there are 3^5 number of possibilities to send elements onto A, B, and C. Since A cannot be empty set, 2^5 number of possibilities must be eliminated. Therefore, $n = 211$.

81. (B) 17

Complementary probability tells us that $1 - \dfrac{3 \cdot 3}{3 \cdot 3 \cdot 3 \cdot 3} = 1 - \dfrac{1}{9} = \dfrac{8}{9}$. Therefore, $m + n = 8 + 9 = 17$.

82. (A) 5

Let seats be $(1, 2, 3), (4, 5, 6), (7, 8)$. The first junior may get inside the first committee with the probability of $\dfrac{3}{8}$. Subsequently, the second junior must get inside the first committee with the probability of $\dfrac{2}{7}$. Likewise, the first junior may get inside the second committee with the probability of $\dfrac{3}{8}$. Hence, the second junior must get inside the second committee with the probability of $\dfrac{2}{7}$. Lastly, the first junior may get inside the third committee with the probability of $\dfrac{2}{8}$. Therefore, the second junior may get inside the third committee with the probability of $\dfrac{1}{7}$. In conclusion,

$$\frac{m}{n} = \frac{3}{8} \times \frac{2}{7} + \frac{3}{8} \times \frac{2}{7} + \frac{2}{8} \times \frac{1}{7} = \frac{1}{4}$$

Thus, $m + n = 5$.

83. (D) 7

According to the condition, $10a + b + 18 = 10b + a$, so $9(b - a) = 18$. Hence, $(a, b) = (1, 3), (2, 4), \cdots, (7, 9)$. There are 7 pairs of (a, b) satisfying the condition. This means that there are 7 $\overline{ab}$s.

84. **(B)** 72

Let $\overline{abc}$ be a three-digit positive integer. According to the condition, we set three possibilities.

1. $a + b + c = 9$: there are 23 triples of (a, b, c) satisfying the equation. Specifically, $\overline{abc} =$ 900, 720, 702, 270, 207, 630, 603, 360, 306, 540, 504, 450, 405, 522, 252, 225, 432, 423, 342, 324, 243, 234, and 333.

2. $a + b + c = 18$: there are 48 triples of (a, b, c) satisfying the equation. Specifically, $\overline{abc} =$ 990, 909, 972, 927, 792, 729, 297, 279, 963, 936, 693, 639, 396, 369, 954, 945, 594, 549, 495, 459, 882, 828, 288, 873, 837, 783, 738, 387, 378, 864, 846, 684, 648, 486, 468, 855, 585, 558, 774, 747, 477, 765, 756, 675, 657, 567, and 576.

3. $a + b + c = 27$: there is 1 triple of (a, b, c) satisfying the equation, i.e., $\overline{abc} = 999$.

Hence, there are 72 three-digit positive integers satisfying the given condition.

Designed and Tailored for
Your Successful Journey on Competition Math

"Don't watch the clock; do what it does. Keep going."

9

9.1 Problem Set

Problem 85.
Keywords: Constructive Probability

If three freshmen, three sophomores, and three juniors are to form three committees of three members each, the probability that each committee has exactly one freshman, one sophomore, and one junior can be written as $\frac{m}{n}$ where m and n are relatively prime positive integers. Determine $m + n$.

(A) 73

(B) 75

(C) 77

(D) 79

(E) 81

Problem 86.
Keywords: Expected Value

If Harry flips a fair coin multiple times in a row, what is the expected number of times he throws a coin in order to have consecutive heads?

(A) 3

(B) 4

(C) 5

(D) 6

(E) 7

Problem 87.
Keywords: Chinese Remainder Theorem, Modular Equation

If a positive integer n has the remainder of 7 when divided by 11 and the remainder of 9 when divided by 13, what is the smallest possible value of n?

(A) 137

(B) 138

(C) 139

(D) 140

(E) 141

Problem 88.

Keywords: Chinese Remainder Theorem, Modular Equation

If a positive integer n has the remainder of 3 when divided by 4, the remainder of 4 when divided by 5, and the remainder of 10 when divided by 11, what is the smallest possible value of n?

(A) 215

(B) 216

(C) 217

(D) 218

(E) 219

Problem 89.

Keywords: Fermat's Little Theorem, Modular Equation

What is the remainder when $5^{5^{5^5}}$ is divided by 6?

(A) 1

(B) 2

(C) 3

(D) 4

(E) 5

Problem 90.

Keywords: Application of Modular Equation

Determine the least positive 2-digit integer n such that $3^n + 4^n$ is divisible by 13.

(A) 11

(B) 13

(C) 15

(D) 17

(E) 19

Problem 91.

Keywords: Diophantine Equation, Modular Equation

If $7x + 4y = 101$ for some non-negative integer pairs (x, y), which of the following is the total number of (x, y) satisfying the given integer equation?

(A) 1

(B) 2

(C) 3

(D) 4

(E) 5

Problem 92.

Keywords: Casework, Diophantine Equation

If $7a + 5b + 3c = 100$, for some non-negative integer triples (a, b, c), determine the total number of (a, b, c) satisfying the given integer equation, assuming that $a \geq 10, 0 \leq b \leq 6$ and $0 \leq c \leq 6$.

(A) 4

(B) 6

(C) 8

(D) 10

(E) 12

Problem 93.

Keywords: Divisor Arithmetic, Probability

Given a set of positive divisors of $2^3 \cdot 3^2 \cdot 5^2 \cdot 7^2$, the probability that an element is a multiple of 30 can be written as $\dfrac{m}{n}$ where m and n are positive integers. Determine $m + n$.

(A) 4

(B) 5

(C) 6

(D) 7

(E) 8

Problem 94.

Keywords: Parity, Primes

If the expression $n^2 - 3n + 2$, for non-negative integer n, always comes out as a prime number, determine the product of possible n-values.

(A) 0

(B) 3

(C) 6

(D) 9

(E) 12

Problem 95.

Keywords: Terminal Zeros, Legendre Function

Which of the following is the number of terminal zeros of 100!?

(A) 18

(B) 20

(C) 22

(D) 24

(E) 26

Problem 96.

Keywords: Base-N expression, Legendre Function

Which of the following is the number of terminal zeros for 100! if written in base 7?

(A) 14

(B) 16

(C) 18

(D) 20

(E) 22

9.2 Solution Manual

85. (D) 79

First, construct $(1,2,3), (4,5,6), (7,8,9)$ for open spots. Let freshmen, sophomores, and juniors be sent onto open spots with the probability of

$$\frac{9}{9} \cdot \frac{6}{8} \cdot \frac{3}{7} \cdot \frac{6}{6} \cdot \frac{4}{5} \cdot \frac{2}{4} \cdot \frac{3}{3} \cdot \frac{2}{2} \cdot \frac{1}{1} = \frac{9}{70}$$

86. (D) 6

Let E be the expected value. Then,

$$\begin{aligned}
E &= \frac{1}{2}(1 + \frac{1}{2}(1) + \frac{1}{2}(1 + E)) + \frac{1}{2}(1 + E) \\
&= \frac{1}{2}(2 + \frac{1}{2}E) + \frac{1}{2} + \frac{1}{2}E \\
&= 1 + \frac{1}{4}E + \frac{1}{2} + \frac{1}{2}E \\
&= \frac{3}{2} + \frac{3}{4}E
\end{aligned}$$

Hence, $E = 6$.

87. (C) 139

Let $n \equiv 7 \pmod{11}$ and $n \equiv 9 \pmod{13}$. Then, $n = 13k + 9$ for some integer k. Hence, $13k + 9 \equiv 7 \pmod{11}$. Hence, $13k \equiv -2 \pmod{11}$, so $k \equiv 10 \pmod{11}$. Therefore, $k = 11q + 10$ for some integer q. Thus, $n = 13(11q + 10) + 9 = 143q + 139$. The smallest possible positive value of n equals 139.

88. (E) 219

Let $n \equiv 3 \pmod{4}$, $n \equiv 4 \pmod{5}$, and $n \equiv 10 \pmod{11}$. In other words, $n \equiv -1 \pmod{220}$. This indicates that $n \equiv 219 \pmod{220}$. The smallest possible value of n equals 219.

89. (E) 5

$$\begin{aligned}
5^{5^{5^5}} &\equiv (-1)^{5^{5^5}} \pmod 6 \\
&\equiv -1 \pmod 6 \\
&\equiv 5 \pmod 6
\end{aligned}$$

90. (C) 15

By inspecting first few cases, notice that $3^3 \equiv 27 \equiv 1 \pmod{13}$ and $4^3 \equiv 64 \equiv -1$ $\pmod{13}$. This implies that $3^3 + 4^3 \equiv 0 \pmod{13}$.

Taking odd power of each term does not change the answer, so we find $(3^3)^5 + (4^3)^5 \equiv 1 + (-1) \equiv 0 \pmod{13}$.

On the other hand, we have $3^{11} + 4^{11} \equiv 3^2 + 4^2 \equiv -1 \pmod{13}$, and $3^{13} + 4^{13} \equiv 3 + 4 \equiv 7 \pmod{13}$, so 15 is the least such n.

91. (C) 3

Using modular arithmetic, we change $7x + 4y = 101$ into $7x + 4y \equiv 101 \pmod{7}$. Hence, $4y \equiv 3 \pmod{7}$, implying $y \equiv -1 \equiv 6 \pmod{7}$. This means that $7x + 4y = 101$ has $(x, y) = (11, 6), (7, 13),$ and $(3, 20)$ as solution pairs, so there are three solutions to the given equation.

92. (B) 6

We perform casework on a.

1. $a = 10 : 5b + 3c = 30$, so $(b, c) = (6, 0), (3, 5)$.

2. $a = 11 : 5b + 3c = 23$, so $(b, c) = (4, 1), (1, 6)$.

3. $a = 12 : 5b + 3c = 16$, so $(b, c) = (2, 2)$.

4. $a = 13 : 5b + 3c = 9$, so $(b, c) = (0, 3)$.

5. $a = 14 : 5b + 3c = 2$, so there is no (b, c) satisfying the given equation.

Hence, there are 6 triples of a, b, and c satisfying $7a + 5b + 3c = 100$ that fits the given condition.

93. (A) 4

First, there are $108(= 4 \times 3 \times 3 \times 3)$ number of positive divisors of $2^3 \cdot 3^2 \cdot 5^2 \cdot 7^2$, because there are four choices to make for powers of 2, three choices to make for powers of 3, 5, and 7, respectively.

Now, in order for an element to be a multiple of 30, at least one power of 2, one power of 3, and one power of 5 should be included. Hence, there are $36(= 3 \times 2 \times 2 \times 3)$ number of integers that fits the condition. Thus, the probability we want can be written as $\dfrac{36}{108} = \dfrac{1}{3}$. The answer must be $4(= 1 + 3)$.

94. (A) 0

Notice that $n^2 - 3n + 2$ is always even. Since $n^2 - 3n + 2 = (n-1)(n-2)$, either $(n-1, n-2) = (\text{even}, \text{odd})$ or $(\text{odd}, \text{even})$.

That being written, $n^2 - 3n + 2$ is even prime, so we conclude that $n^2 - 3n + 2 = 2$. Thus, $n^2 - 3n = n(n-3) = 0$. The product of $n = 0$ and $n = 3$ equals 0.

95. (D) 24

Terminal zeros are determined by the number of 2s and that of 5s. Since there are less number of 5s in 100!, we compute the number of 5s as

$$\left\lfloor \frac{100}{5} \right\rfloor + \left\lfloor \frac{100}{5^2} \right\rfloor = 20 + 4 = 24$$

Hence, there are 24 terminal zeros in the expression.

96. (B) 16

Terminal zeros in base 7 depends on the powers of 7 in 100!. Hence, we capture the number of 7s in 100! as

$$\left\lfloor \frac{100}{7} \right\rfloor + \left\lfloor \frac{100}{49} \right\rfloor = 14 + 2 = 16$$

Thus, there are 16 terminal zeros for 100! in base 7 expression.

Designed and Tailored for
Your Successful Journey on Competition Math

"Exams are not just a test of knowledge,
but a test of your perseverance and dedication."

10

10.1 Problem Set

Problem 97.

Keywords: Modular Equation, Divisibility

If $n^2 + 2n - 1$ is divisible by $n - 1$ for some non-negative integers, determine the total number of n-values.

(A) 2

(B) 3

(C) 4

(D) 5

(E) 6

Problem 98.

Keywords: Definition of Divisors, Casework

If $n + 3$ is divisible by $n^2 + 2n - 1$ for some non-negative integer n, determine the sum of all possible n-values.

(A) 1

(B) 2

(C) 3

(D) 4

(E) 5

Problem 99.

Keywords: Greatest Common Divisor

What is the greatest common divisor of $7!$ and $\dfrac{8!}{3!}$?

(A) 1200

(B) 1240

(C) 1440

(D) 1680

(E) 1840

Problem 100.

Keywords: Greatest Common Divisor, Divisor Arithmetic

Which of the following is the number of positive *even* divisors of 10!.

(A) 20

(B) 60

(C) 120

(D) 180

(E) 240

Problem 101.

Keywords: Modular Arithmetic

Which of the following is the units digit of the sum $1! + 2! + 3! + \cdots + 1000!$?

(A) 0

(B) 1

(C) 2

(D) 3

(E) 4

Problem 102.

Keywords: P-adic Expression, Legendre Function

Determine the number of terminal zeros of $\binom{20}{10}$.

(A) 0

(B) 1

(C) 2

(D) 3

(E) 4

Problem 103.

Keywords: Least Common Multiple

Which of the following is the number of all positive integers n for which $\text{lcm}(n, 40) = 120$?

(A) 4

(B) 6

(C) 8

(D) 10

(E) 12

Problem 104.

Keywords: 3D Geometry, Labeling, Expressions

Given a $n \times n \times n$ cube, for some integer n, which of the following could be the number of unit cubes on the original cube's surfaces?

(A) 142

(B) 146

(C) 148

(D) 152

(E) 154

Problem 105.

Keywords: Casework, Labeling, Digits

In how many three-digit positive integers N will have the sum of $N = \overline{abc}$ and its digit-reversed $N' = \overline{cba}$ as a three-digit perfect square?

(A) 7

(B) 8

(C) 10

(D) 12

(E) 14

Problem 106.

Keywords: Labeling, Integer Equations

In how many *distinct* ways can 100 be written as a sum of at least two consecutive positive integers? (For example, 10 has only one way of summation, i.e., $1 + 2 + 3 + 4 = 10$.)

(A) 0

(B) 1

(C) 2

(D) 3

(E) 4

Problem 107.

Keywords: Arithmetic Sequence, Arithmetic Series, Integer Inequality

If seven positive integers form an arithmetic sequence, including a trivial one, the sum of all terms in this finite sequence is 1001. How many different arithmetic sequences can be made, in total, satisfying the given condition?

(A) 88

(B) 89

(C) 90

(D) 91

(E) 92

Problem 108.

Keywords: Chinese Remainder Theorem, Terminal Zeros

17! has 3 terminal zeros. What is the first non-zero digit in the decimal expansion of 17! read from right to left? (For example, 1234000 has 4 as its first non-zero digit read from right to left.)

(A) 2

(B) 4

(C) 5

(D) 6

(E) 8

10.2   Solution Manual

97. (B) 3

Notice that $n \equiv 1 \pmod{n-1}$. Thus, $n^2 + 2n - 1 \equiv 1^2 + 2(1) - 1 \equiv 2 \pmod{n-1}$. This implies that $n - 1$ is either 2, -2, 1, or -1. Therefore, $n = 2, 0, 3$, or -1. Since we only count non-negative integers, there are three possible values of n.

98. (A) 1

According to the given condition, we set $|n^2 + 2n - 1| \leq |n + 3|$. Since $n \geq 0$, we set $|n^2 + 2n - 1| \leq n + 3$. For $n > 1$, $n^2 + 2n - 1 \leq n + 3$ implies that $n^2 + n - 4 \leq 0$. This makes no sense, so we look at $n = 0$ and $n = 1$.

If $n = 0$, then we conclude that 3 is divisible by -1. If $n = 1$, we conclude that 4 is divisible by 2. Hence, the sum of these two values equals 1.

99. (D) 1680

Notice that $7! = 42 \cdot 5!$ and $\dfrac{8!}{3!} = 56 \cdot 5!$. Hence, we need to find out the greatest common divisor of 42 and 56, which is 14. Hence, the greatest common divisor of the original two numbers equals $14(5!) = 14(120) = 1680$.

100. (E) 240

Prime factorization of $10!$ equals $2^8 \cdot 3^4 \cdot 5^2 \cdot 7^1$. Hence, the number of even divisors can be computed by counting the number of possible powers of 2, 3, 5 and 7, respectively.

- Powers of 2 : choose one out of $\{2^1, 2^2, \cdots, 2^8\}$ in 8 different ways.

- Powers of 3 : choose one out of $\{3^0, 3^1, \cdots, 3^4\}$ in 5 different ways.

- Powers of 5 : choose one out of $\{5^0, 5^1, 5^2\}$ in 3 different ways.

- Powers of 7 : choose one out of $\{7^0, 7^1\}$ in 2 different ways.

Hence, there are $240(= 8 \times 5 \times 3 \times 2)$ even divisors of $10!$.

101. (D) 3

$$1! + 2! + 3! + 4! + 5! + \cdots + 1000! \equiv 1! + 2! + 3! + 4! + 0 + \cdots + 0 \pmod{10}$$
$$\equiv 1 + 2 + 6 + 4 \pmod{10}$$
$$\equiv 3 \pmod{10}$$

102. (A) 0

By definition, $\binom{20}{10} = \frac{20!}{10!10!}$. All we need to find out is the powers of 5. In 20!, there are $\left\lfloor \frac{20}{5} \right\rfloor = 4$ number of 5s. In 10!, there are $\left\lfloor \frac{20}{10} \right\rfloor = 2$ number of 5s. This implies that $\frac{20!}{10!10!} = \frac{5^4 \cdot K_1}{(5^2 \cdot K_2)^2}$ for some integer K_1 and K_2 not divisible by 5, so we conclude that there is no terminal zero in the given expression.

103. (C) 8

Remember that the least common multiple takes maximum powers of each prime that appears. Factorize 40 and 120 to see that $40 = 2^3 \cdot 5$ and $120 = 2^3 \cdot 3 \cdot 5$. Hence, the only primes that appear in n are 2, 3, and 5.

Let $n = 2^a 3^b 5^c$. Then, $max(a, 3) = 3$ implies that $a \in \{0, 1, 2, 3\}$. Likewise, $max(b, 0) = 1$ implies that $b = 1$. Lastly, $max(c, 1) = 1$ implies that $c \in \{0, 1\}$. Therefore, there are $8(= 4 \times 1 \times 2)$ number of ns.

104. (D) 152

The number of unit cubes on the original cube's surfaces can be found by $n^3 - (n-2)^3$.

$$
\begin{aligned}
n^3 - (n-2)^3 &= (n - (n-2))(n^2 + n(n-2) + (n-2)^2) \\
&= 2(n^2 + n^2 - 2n + n^2 - 4n + 4) \\
&= 2(3n^2 - 6n + 4)
\end{aligned}
$$

Now, we use the answer choices in the following fashion.

1. $2(3n^2 - 6n + 4) = 142$ implies $3n^2 - 6n + 4 = 71$. Since $3n(n-2) = 67$, there is no integer value of n.

2. $2(3n^2 - 6n + 4) = 146$ implies $3n^2 - 6n + 4 = 73$. Since $3n(n-2) = 69$, we get $n(n-2) = 23$. There is no integer value of n.

3. $2(3n^2 - 6n + 4) = 148$ implies $3n^2 - 6n + 4 = 74$. Since $3n(n-2) = 70$, there is no integer value of n.

4. $2(3n^2 - 6n + 4) = 152$ implies $3n^2 - 6n + 4 = 76$. Since $3n(n-2) = 72$, we get $n(n-2) = 24$, so $n^2 - 2n - 24 = (n-6)(n+4) = 0$, Thus, $n = 6$.

5. $2(3n^2 - 6n + 4) = 154$ implies $3n^2 - 6n + 4 = 77$. Since $3n(n-2) = 73$, there is no integer value of n.

105. (A) 7

The sum of $\overline{abc}$ and $\overline{cba}$ can be rewritten as $101(a+c) + 20b$, which should be one of the values : $225, 256, 289, 324, 361, 400, 441, 484, 529, 576, 625, 676, 729, 784, 841, 900$ and 961. As we perform casework on $a+c$, we get

1. $a+c=2$: there is no value of b since none of the perfect square ends with 2.

2. $a+c=3$: there is no value of b since none of the perfect square ends with 3.

3. $a+c=4$: either $20b = 80$ or $20b = 380$. Since $b \le 9$, we conclude that $b=4$.

4. $a+c=5$: we have $20b = 120$, so $b=6$.

5. $a+c=6$: there is no value of b since $20b = 70$ does not result in integer value of b.

6. $a+c=7$: there is no value of b since none of the perfect square ends with 7.

7. $a+c=8$: there is no value of b since none of the perfect square ends with 8.

8. $a+c=9$: there is no value of b since 961 does not end with 9 as its units digit.

Hence, we conclude that $N = \overline{abc}$ is either $143, 341, 164, 461, 263, 362$ and 242.

106. (C) 2

Let $100 = (n+1) + (n+2) + \cdots + (n+k)$ for $n \ge 0$ and $k \ge 2$. Then, we can rearrange it into $200 = 2kn + k(k+1) = k(2n+k+1)$. Notice that $2n+k+1 \ge k$. Thus, we write down all possible cases such as

$$k(2n+k+1) = 200$$
$$2(100) = 200$$
$$4(50) = 200$$
$$5(40) = 200$$
$$8(25) = 200$$
$$10(20) = 200$$

If k is even, then $2n+k+1$ must be odd. Hence, at $k=8$, $2n+8+1 = 25$, so $2n = 16$. This implies that $9 + 10 + 11 + \cdots + 16 = 100$. On the other hand, if k is odd, then $2n+k+1$ must be even. Hence, at $k=5$, $2n+5+1 = 40$, so $n=17$. This implies that $18 + 19 + 20 + 21 + 22 = 100$. Therefore, there are 2 ways of summing at least two consecutive positive integers to get 100.

107. (B) 89

Let k be the middle term in the arithmetic sequence such that
$\{k - 3d, k - 2d, k - d, k, k + d, k + 2d, k + 3d\}$. Notice that the sum equals $7k = 1001$, indicating that $k = 143$. It is easy to see that d is an integer. Let's assume that the sequence is increasing. Then, $d > 0$. In this case, $143 - 3d > 0$ implies that $44 \geq d$. This shows that $0 < d \leq 44$. There are 44 possible values of d when the sequence is increasing. Symmetrically, there are 44 possible values of d when the sequence is decreasing. Lastly, one should not forget about when $d = 0$. Thus, there are 89 possible arithmetic sequences satisfying the given condition.

108. (D) 6

Notice that $17! = 2^{15} \cdot 3^6 \cdot 5^3 \cdot 7^2 \cdot 11^1 \cdot 13^1 \cdot 17^1$. We take out 4 terminal zeros from $17!$ to get $2^{12} \cdot 3^6 \cdot 7^2 \cdot 11^1 \cdot 13^1 \cdot 17^1$. Now, let it be called as N.

Then, $N \equiv 0 \pmod 2$, for obvious reason. On the other hand, for mod 5,

$$2^{12} \cdot 3^6 \cdot 7^2 \cdot 11^1 \cdot 13^1 \cdot 17^1 \equiv 1 \cdot (-1) \cdot (-1) \cdot 1 \cdot 3 \cdot 2 \pmod 5$$
$$\equiv 1 \pmod 5$$

This implies that $N \equiv 0 \pmod 2$ and $N \equiv 1 \pmod 5$. By Chinese Remainder Theorem, we get $N \equiv 6 \pmod{10}$. Hence, the first non-zero digit must be 6.

 # List of Interesting Polyhedron

Rhombicuboctahedron: The rhombicuboctahedron is a fascinating polyhedron with its mix of square and triangular faces. Its name alone can bring a smile to people's faces due to its complexity and tongue-twisting nature.

Truncated Icosahedron: This polyhedron is famously known as the shape of a traditional soccer ball. Its spherical appearance made up of hexagons and pentagons is both recognizable and aesthetically pleasing.

Dodecahedron: The dodecahedron is another polyhedron that captures attention due to its symmetrical beauty. Its twelve regular pentagonal faces give it a pleasing and harmonious appearance.

Stellated Dodecahedron: By extending the faces of a dodecahedron outward, you get the stellated dodecahedron. Its star-like appearance makes it visually striking and often intriguing to mathematicians and artists alike.

Truncated Tetrahedron: This polyhedron results from cutting off the corners of a tetrahedron. Its triangular and hexagonal faces can create interesting patterns and visual effects.

Great Rhombicosidodecahedron: With its mix of faces including triangles, squares, and pentagons, this polyhedron is a complex and visually captivating shape that can inspire wonder and curiosity.

Snub Cube: The snub cube is derived from the cube by adding pyramids to each face. Its asymmetrical yet balanced appearance can be both surprising and delightful to those who encounter it.

Icosidodecahedron: Combining the properties of an icosahedron and a dodecahedron, this polyhedron features both triangular and pentagonal faces arranged in a symmetrical and harmonious manner.

Designed and Tailored for
Your Successful Journey on Competition Math

" Stay focused, stay positive, and remember why you started. "

11

11.1 Problem Set

Problem 109.

Keywords: Equilateral Triangle, Label, Segment Addition Postulate

Given a square $ABCD$, if ABE is an equilateral triangle such that E is inside the square, the ratio between the area of ABE and that of CDE can be written as $a\sqrt{b} + c$ for positive integers a, b, and c such that b is a square-free integer. Determine $a + b + c$.

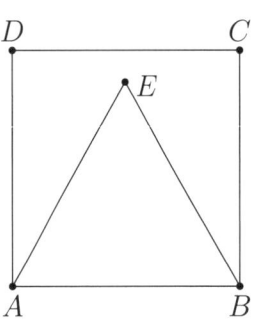

(A) 6   (B) 7   (C) 8   (D) 9   (E) 10

Problem 110.

Keywords: Constructive Geometry, Special Right Triangle, Isosceles Triangle

Given a right triangle ABC such that $\angle B$ is right, if $m\angle A = 75°$, then $\tan(A)$ can be written as $a + \sqrt{b}$ where a and b are positive integers. Determine $a + b$. (You do not need to know about trigonometry to solve for this problem.)

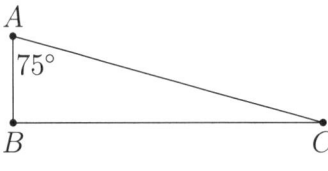

(A) 5   (B) 6   (C) 7   (D) 11   (E) 18

Problem 111.

Keywords: Pythagorean Theorem, Heron's Formula

Given a triangle with side length 5, 6 and 7, the area of the triangle can be written as $a\sqrt{a}$ where a is a square-free positive integer. Determine a.

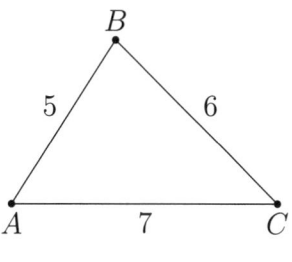

(A) 3   (B) 4   (C) 5   (D) 6   (E) 7

Problem 112.

Keywords: Pythagorean Theorem, Invariance

If a rhombus with side length of 10 and with its longest diagonal of length 16, there exists a circle inscribed inside the rhombus. The circumference of this circle can be written as $\dfrac{m}{n}\pi$ where m and n are relatively prime positive integers. Determine $m + n$.

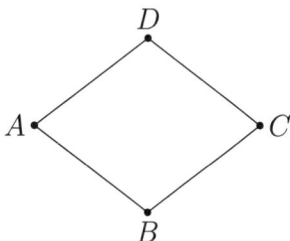

(A) 45   (B) 47   (C) 49   (D) 51   (E) 53

Problem 113.

Keywords: Power of Points, Similar Figures, Cyclic Quadrilateral

If a chord $\overline{AB}$ and another chord $\overline{CD}$ intersect at X inside the same circle such that $AX = 4$, $BX = 6$, and $CX = 8$, find the length DX.

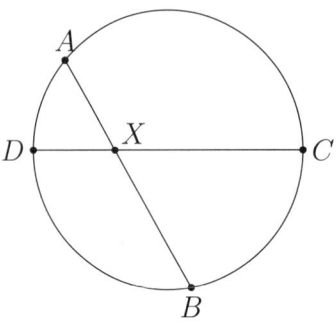

(A) 1   (B) 2   (C) 3   (D) 4   (E) 5

Problem 114.

Keywords: Pythagorean Theorem, Invariance, Coordinate Geometry

Given $y = 2x + 11$ and $y = 2x + 15$, the square of the distance between the two parallel lines can be written as $\dfrac{m}{n}$ where m and n are relatively prime positive integers. Determine $m + n$.

(A) 19

(B) 21

(C) 23

(D) 25

(E) 27

Problem 115.

Keywords: Coordinate Geometry, Vector, Pythagorean Theorem, Invariance

If $y = 7x + 11$ and the point $(11, 10)$ is d units away from each other, then the exact value of d^2 can be written as $\frac{m}{n}$ where m and n are relatively prime positive integers. Determine the exact value of n.

(A) 9

(B) 10

(C) 19

(D) 25

(E) 50

Problem 116.

Keywords: Isosceles Triangle, Labeling, Pythagorean Theorem

The circumradius of an isosceles triangle with side lengths 10, 10 and 12 can be written as $\frac{m}{n}$ where m and n are relatively prime positive integers. Determine $m + n$.

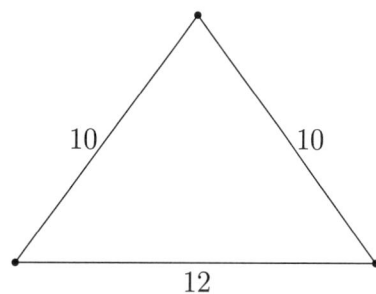

(A) 21   (B) 23   (C) 25   (D) 27   (E) 29

Problem 117.

Keywords: Pythagorean Theorem, Invariance, British Flag Theorem

Given a rectangle $ABCD$ where there exists a point P inside the rectangle. If $PA = 3$, $PB = 4$ and $PC = 5$, then determine PD^2.

(A) 16

(B) 18

(C) 19

(D) 20

(E) 21

Problem 118.

Keywords: Orthocenter, Similar Triangles

Given an acute triangle ABC, if the altitude from C to $\overline{AB}$ and that from A to $\overline{BC}$ intersect at H, let $AH = CH = 4$ and $AC = 6$. The perimeter of the triangle ABC can be written as $\dfrac{a + b\sqrt{c}}{d}$ where a, b, c, and d are positive integers, and c is a square-free integer. Determine $a + b + c + d$.

(A) 76

(B) 78

(C) 80

(D) 82

(E) 84

Problem 119.

Keywords: Externally Tangent Circles, Right Triangle

A diagram below shows a circle with radius 10 which contains two circles with radius 5 tangent to each other. There exists the smallest circle, shown in the figure, tangent to the three original circles. The radius of the smallest circle can be written as $\frac{m}{n}$ where m and n are relatively prime positive integers. Determine $m + n$.

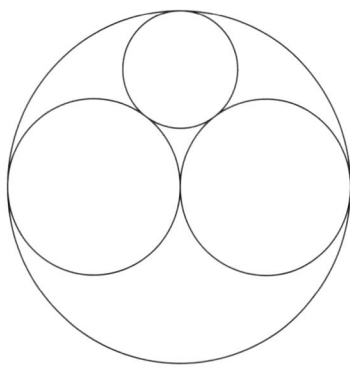

(A) 11   (B) 12   (C) 13   (D) 14   (E) 15

Problem 120.

Keywords: Labeling, Similar Figures, Right Triangle

Given a right triangle ABC with $AB = 3$, $BC = 4$, and $AC = 5$, there exist two squares inscribed inside the triangle such that at least one of its side is on the triangle sides, as shown in the figure below. The difference in their side lengths can be written as $\frac{m}{n}$ where m and n are relatively prime positive integers. Determine $m + n$.

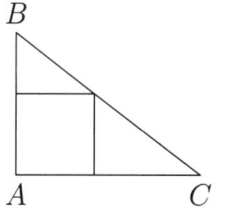

(A) 281   (B) 283   (C) 285   (D) 287   (E) 289

11.2 Solution Manual

109. (C) 8

Look at the following figure.

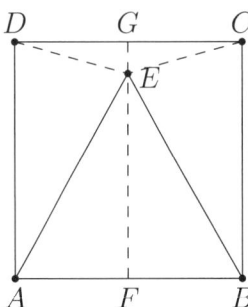

Without loss of generality, let's assume that $AB = BC = CD = AD = 2$. Then, it is easy to check that $AE = BE = 2$. The area of ABE and that of CDE share the same base $AB = CD$, so we must decide the height ratio. Let F and G be the point of perpendicular foot from E to $\overline{AB}$ and $\overline{CD}$, respectively.

By special right triangle $30° - 60° - 90°$, we conclude that $EF = \sqrt{3}$. Since $GE + EF = 2$ by segment-addition postulate, we conclude that $GE = 2 - EF = 2 - \sqrt{3}$. Thus, the ratio we want can be written as $\dfrac{\sqrt{3}}{2 - \sqrt{3}} = \dfrac{\sqrt{3}(2 + \sqrt{3})}{(2 - \sqrt{3})(2 + \sqrt{3})} = 2\sqrt{3} + 3$. Therefore, $a + b + c = 2 + 3 + 3 = 8$.

110. (A) 5

Look at the following figure.

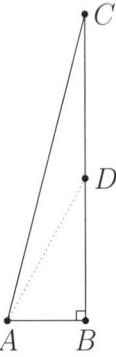

Assume that $m\angle A = 75°$. Then, we choose D on $\overline{BC}$ such that $m\angle BAD = 60°$. Hence, $m\angle DAC = m\angle DCA = 15°$. Without loss of generality, assume that $AB = 1$. Then, $BD = \sqrt{3}$ and $AD = 2$, using special right triangle property. Since $\triangle ADC$ is isosceles, we conclude that $CD = AD = 2$. Thus,

$$\tan(75°) = \frac{BC}{AB} = 2 + \sqrt{3}.$$

111. (D) 6

Look at the following figure.

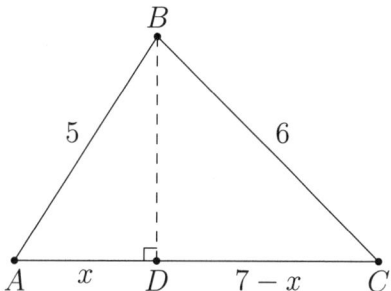

According to Pythagorean Theorem,

$$6^2 - 5^2 = (7-x)^2 - x^2$$
$$36 - 25 = (49 - 14x + x^2) - x^2$$
$$11 = 49 - 14x$$
$$-38 = -14x$$
$$\frac{19}{7} = x$$

Using Pythagorean Theorem once more, we get

$$BD^2 = AB^2 - AD^2$$
$$= 5^2 - \left(\frac{19}{7}\right)^2$$
$$= (5 - \frac{19}{7})(5 + \frac{19}{7})$$
$$= (\frac{16}{7})(\frac{54}{7})$$
$$BD = \frac{12}{7}\sqrt{6}$$

Hence, the area of triangle ABC equals $\frac{1}{2} \times 7 \times \frac{12}{7}\sqrt{6} = 6\sqrt{6}$.

On the other hand, if one uses Heron's formula, then

1. $s = \dfrac{5 + 6 + 7}{2} = \dfrac{18}{2} = 9.$

2. $[ABC] = \sqrt{s(s-5)(s-6)(s-7)} = \sqrt{9 \cdot 4 \cdot 3 \cdot 2} = 6\sqrt{6}.$

Therefore, we conclude that $[ABC] = 6\sqrt{6} = a\sqrt{a}$, so $a = 6$.

112. (E) 53

Look at the following figure.

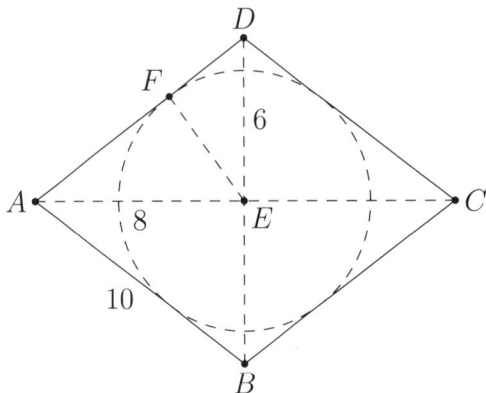

As one can see from the figure, let E be the intersection point between $\overline{AC}$ and $\overline{BD}$. Then, $DE = BE = 6$ and $AE = CE = 8$, according to a rhombus property. It is easy to check that $AB = BC = CD = DA = 10$ by special right triangle property. Since $[AED]$ is invariant, we solve

$$\frac{1}{2} \times 10 \times EF = \frac{1}{2} \times 8 \times 6$$

$$10 \times EF = 48$$

$$EF = \frac{24}{5}$$

Hence, the circumference of the circle is $\frac{48}{5}\pi$, so $m + n = 48 + 5 = 53$.

113. (C) 3

Look at the following figure.

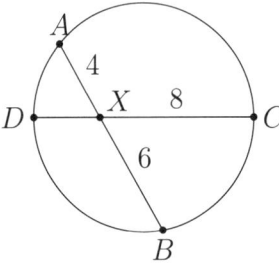

According to the power of points,

$$AX \times BX = CX \times DX$$

$$4 \times 6 = 8 \times DX$$

$$24 = 8DX$$

$$3 = DX$$

114. (B) 21

Let d be the distance between the line $y = 2x + 11$ and $y = 2x + 15$. Look at the following figure.

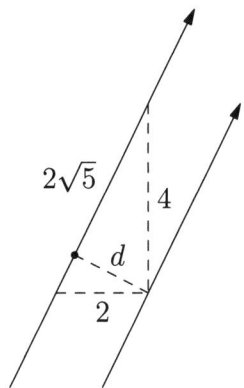

According to the invariance condition, $\frac{1}{2} \times 2 \times 4 = \frac{1}{2} \times 2\sqrt{5} \times d$, so $d = \frac{4}{\sqrt{5}}$. Hence, $d^2 = \frac{16}{5}$, so $m + n = 16 + 5 = 21$.

115. (D) 25

We use the same approach as in problem 114. Look at the following figure.

According to the figure, $(11 - 7k, 10 + k)$ will stay on the graph of $y = 7x + 11$. Hence,

$$10 + k = 7(11 - 7k) + 11$$
$$10 + k = 77 - 49k + 11$$
$$10 + k = 88 - 49k$$
$$50k = 78$$
$$k = \frac{39}{25}$$

Hence, the distance d can be written as $\sqrt{50}k = \sqrt{50}\frac{39}{25}$, so $d^2 = \frac{2 \cdot 39^2}{25}$. Thus, $n = 25$.

116. (E) 29

Look at the following figure.

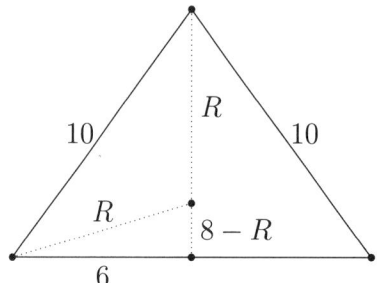

As one can see from the figure, we use Pythagorean Theorem, i.e.,

$$R^2 = (8 - R)^2 + 6^2$$
$$R^2 = 64 - 16R + R^2 + 36$$
$$16R = 100$$
$$R = \frac{100}{16}$$
$$= \frac{25}{4}$$

Hence, $m + n = 25 + 4 = 29$.

117. (B) 18

Look at the following figure. This is a famous British Flag theorem.

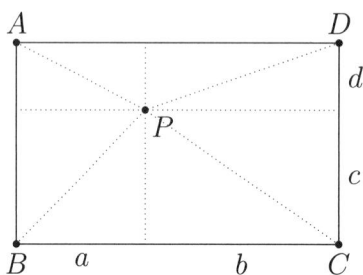

It is easy to check that $PA^2 = a^2 + d^2$, $PB^2 = a^2 + c^2$, $PC^2 = b^2 + c^2$, and $PD^2 = b^2 + d^2$. Hence,

$$PA^2 + PC^2 = PB^2 + PD^2$$
$$(a^2 + d^2) + (b^2 + c^2) = (a^2 + c^2) + (b^2 + d^2)$$
$$3^2 + 5^2 = 4^2 + PD^2$$
$$9 + 25 = 16 + PD^2$$
$$34 = 16 + PD^2$$
$$18 = PD^2$$

118. (C) 80

Look at the following figure.

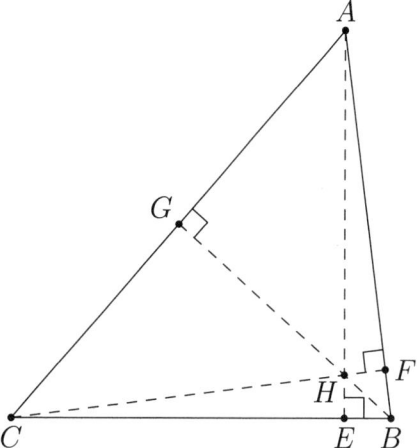

As shown in the figure above, let E, F, and G be the perpendicular feet from vertices to the opposite sides, respectively. Since $AH = HC$, we conclude that $\triangle AHC$ is isosceles. Hence, G must be the midpoint of $\overline{AC}$. According to Pythagorean Theorem, we conclude that $AG = 3$, $GH = \sqrt{7}$ and $AH = 4$.

Since $\triangle AGH \sim \triangle AEC$, we retrieve $CE = AF = \dfrac{3\sqrt{7}}{2}$ and $AE = CF = 4\dfrac{1}{2}$. Thus, $EH = FH = \dfrac{1}{2}$. Also, notice that $\triangle AGH \sim \triangle BEH$, so $AG : GH = BE : EH$. This implies that $EH = \dfrac{3\sqrt{7}}{14}$.

Therefore, the perimeter of ABC equals $AB + BC + AC = \dfrac{24\sqrt{7}}{7} + 6 = \dfrac{42 + 24\sqrt{7}}{7}$. Hence, $a + b + c + d = 42 + 24 + 7 + 7 = 80$.

119. (C) 13

Look at the following figure.

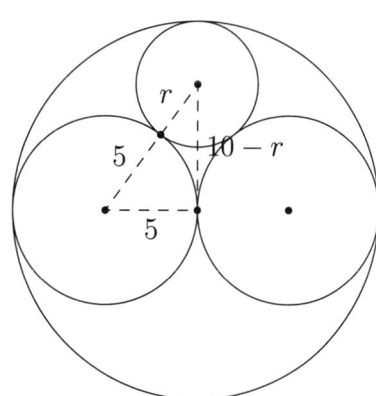

According to Pythagorean Theorem, we set $(5 + r)^2 = (10 - r)^2 + 5^2$, so $25 + 10r + r^2 = 100 - 20r + r^2 + 25$, implying $r = \dfrac{10}{3}$. Thus, $m + n = 10 + 3 = 13$.

120. (B) 283

Look at the following figure.

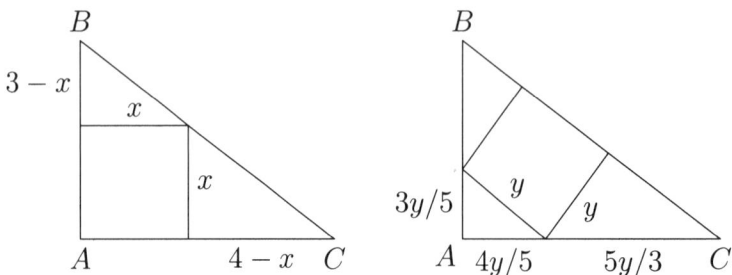

For the first triangle, it is easy to check that

$$\frac{3-x}{x} = \frac{x}{4-x}$$
$$= \frac{3}{4}$$
$$12 - 4x = 3x$$
$$12 = 7x$$
$$\frac{12}{7} = x$$

On the other hand, for the second triangle, we can set

$$\frac{4y}{5} + \frac{5y}{3} = 4$$
$$\frac{37}{15}y = 4$$
$$y = \frac{60}{37}$$

Hence, the difference of their side lengths equals $\left| \frac{60}{37} - \frac{12}{7} \right| = \frac{24}{259}$.

Designed and Tailored for
Your Successful Journey on Competition Math

"Great things never come from comfort zones."

12

12.1 Problem Set

Problem 121.

Keywords: Labeling, Orthocenter, Similar Figures

Let ABC be an acute triangle where $\overline{AE}$ is the altitude from A to $\overline{BC}$ and $\overline{BD}$ is the altitude from B to $\overline{AC}$. Let the intersection point between $\overline{AE}$ and $\overline{BD}$ be H. If $DH = 2$, $BH = 5$ and $EH = 4$, then AB^2 can be written as $\dfrac{m}{n}$ where m and n are relatively prime positive integers. Determine $m + n$.

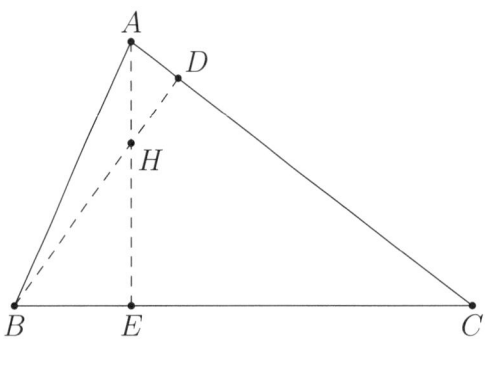

(A) 206   (B) 207   (C) 208   (D) 209   (E) 210

Problem 122.

Keywords: Labeling, Laws of Sines

Given a regular dodecahedron, let A be one of the vertices. Let B, C, and D be adjacent vertices to A. Assuming $AB = AC = AD = 4$, the perimeter of BCD can be written as $a + a\sqrt{b}$ where a and b are square-free integers. Determine $a + b$.

(A) 11   (B) 12   (C) 13   (D) 14   (E) 15

Problem 123.

Keywords: Pythagorean Theorem, Heron's Formula

Let $ABCD$ be a cyclic quadrilateral with $AB = 5$, $BC = 5$, $CD = 10$, and $AD = 3$. If lines $\overline{AB}$ and $\overline{CD}$ meet at a point E, the perimeter of EBC can be written as $\dfrac{m}{n}$ where m and n are relatively prime positive integers. Determine $m + n$.

(A) 83

(B) 84

(C) 85

(D) 86

(E) 87

Problem 124.

Keywords: Pythagorean Theorem, Invariance

Given an equilateral triangle ABC, where D, E, and F are points on $\overline{BC}$, $\overline{AC}$, and $\overline{AB}$ such that $\dfrac{CD}{BD} = \dfrac{AE}{CE} = \dfrac{BF}{AF} = \dfrac{1}{2}$. If $\overline{AD}$ and $\overline{BE}$ intersect at X, $\overline{BE}$ and $\overline{CF}$ intersect at Y and $\overline{CF}$ and $\overline{AD}$ intersect at Z. Which of the following ratio of the areas of $\triangle ABC$ and $\triangle XYZ$?

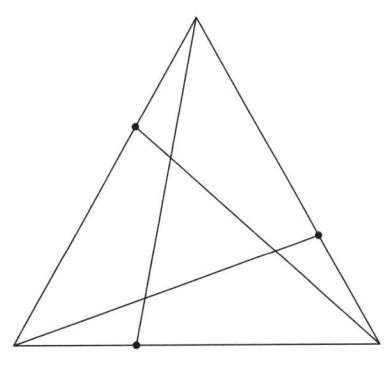

(A) 5   (B) 7   (C) 9   (D) 11   (E) 13

Problem 125.

Keywords: Power of Points, Similar Figures, Pythagorean Theorem

Circle centered at O has a diameter of length 15. Given a diameter $\overline{AB}$, there exists a point C off the circle such that $\overline{AC}$ is tangent to the circle and $\overline{BC}$ intersects the circle at point D with $BD = 12$. The length AC can be written as $\dfrac{m}{n}$ where m and n are relatively prime positive integers. Determine $m + n$.

(A) 49

(B) 50

(C) 51

(D) 52

(E) 53

Problem 126.

Keywords: Externally Tangent Circles

Given an isosceles trapezoid $ABCD$ where $AB > CD$, if there are two semicircles drawn inside the figure whose diameters are $\overline{BC}$ and $\overline{AD}$ with the length of 10, the circles are externally tangent. Which of the following is the perimeter of $ABCD$?

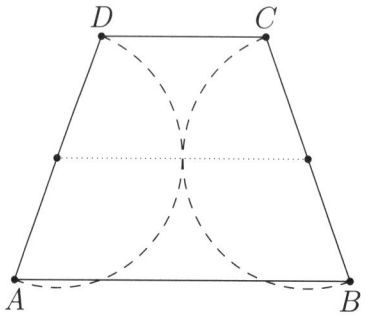

(A) 30   (B) 40   (C) 50   (D) 60   (E) 70

Problem 127.

Keywords: Similar Figures, Right Triangle

An altitude to the hypotenuse of a right triangle produces segments of length 4 and 6. Determine the exact area of the triangle.

(A) $5\sqrt{6}$

(B) $7\sqrt{6}$

(C) $9\sqrt{6}$

(D) $10\sqrt{6}$

(E) $12\sqrt{6}$

Problem 128.

Keywords: Labeling, Similar Figures, Right Triangle

Which of the following is the area of the quadrilateral $XCYF$ in the regular hexagon of side length 4, as shown in the figure below? Assume that X and Y are midpoints of $\overline{AB}$ and $\overline{ED}$, respectively.

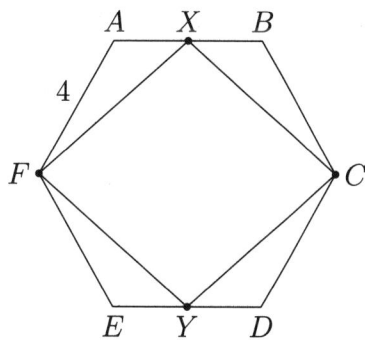

(A) $15\sqrt{3}$ (B) $16\sqrt{3}$ (C) $17\sqrt{3}$ (D) $18\sqrt{3}$ (E) $19\sqrt{3}$

Problem 129.

Keywords: Coordinate Geometry, Perpendicular Bisector

There are two circles which pass through the points $(7, 1)$ and $(3, 4)$, both of which are tangent to the x-axis. The sum of the radii can be written as $\dfrac{m}{n}$ where m and n are relatively prime positive integers. Determine $m + n$.

(A) 130

(B) 132

(C) 134

(D) 136

(E) 138

Problem 130.

Keywords: Coordinate Geometry, Shoelace Theorem

If $A(4, 8)$, $B(7, 12)$, $C(6, 10)$ and D are the four vertices of parallelogram $ABCD$, which of the following is the area of $ABCD$?

(A) 1

(B) 2

(C) 3

(D) 4

(E) 5

Problem 131.

Keywords: Regular Hexagon, Pythagorean Theorem, Chord, Inscribed Angle and Central Angle

A hexagon inscribed in a circle has three lengths $AB = CD = EF = 4$ and $BC = DE = AF = 6$. The area of triangle ACE can be written as $a\sqrt{b}$ where a and b are square-free integers. Determine $a + b$.

(A) 19

(B) 20

(C) 21

(D) 22

(E) 23

Problem 132.

Keywords: Incircle, Similar Figures

Given a triangle ABC with incircle O with the side lengths of 6, 7, and 8. Let r be the inradius. Draw a line passing through O, parallel to $\overline{BC}$, and label the intersection points as B_A and C_A, respectively along the side $\overline{AB}$ and $\overline{AC}$. Let r_A be the inradius of the triangle AB_AC_A. Similarly, define r_B and r_C. The ratio of $\dfrac{r_A + r_B + r_C}{r}$ can be written as an integer value of n. Find n.

(A) 1   (B) 2   (C) 3   (D) 4   (E) 5

12.2 Solution Manual

121. (D) 209

Triangle BHE and AHD are similar, so $\dfrac{AD}{2} = \dfrac{BE}{HE} = \dfrac{3}{4}$. This implies that $AD = 1.5$.

By Pythagorean Theorem, $AD^2 + BD^2 = 2.25 + 49 = 51.25$. Thus, $AB^2 = 51\dfrac{1}{4} = \dfrac{205}{4}$. Thus, $m + n = 209$.

122. (A) 11

Notice that $\angle BAC = 108°$. By the law of cosines,
$BC^2 = CD^2 = BD^2 = 4^2 + 4^2 - 2(4)(4)\cos(108°) = 32 + 32\cos(72°)$. Hence,
$BC^2 = 24 + 8\sqrt{5}$. Since $BC^2 = 24 + 2\sqrt{80}$, we conclude that
$BC = \sqrt{4} + \sqrt{20} = 2 + 2\sqrt{5}$. Therefore, $BC + CD + BC = 3(2 + 2\sqrt{5}) = 6 + 6\sqrt{5}$.

123. (E) 87

Let $EA = a$ and $ED = b$. Then, by similarity ratio, we get

$$\frac{a}{b+10} = \frac{b}{a+5} = \frac{3}{5}$$

Hence, $5a = 3b + 30$ and $5b = 3a + 15$. Since $5a - 3b = 30$ and $-3a + 5b = 15$, we get $2a + 2b = 45$. The perimeter of EBC equals

$$a + b + 5 + 10 + 5 = a + b + 20 = \frac{45}{2} + 20 = \frac{85}{2}.$$

124. (B) 7

Let $AB = BC = CA = 3k$. Then, $AE = BF = CD = k$. The laws of cosines states that $BE^2 = AD^2 = CF^2 = k^2 + (3k)^2 - 2(3k)(k)\cos(60°) = 7k^2$. Hence, $BE = AD = CF = \sqrt{7}k$.

Using Menelaus Theorem or Mass Point Geometry, we check that
$AX : XD = BY : YE = CZ : ZF = 3 : 4$. Likewise,
$AZ : DZ = CY : FY = BX : XE = 6 : 1$. Hence,
$AX : XZ : XD = CZ : ZY : YF = BY : YX : XE = 3 : 3 : 1$. Therefore,
$XY = YZ = ZX = \dfrac{3}{7}\sqrt{7}k$.

Since the area ratio is the square of length ratio, we conclude that
$ABC : XYZ = 9 : \dfrac{9}{7} = 7 : 1$.

125. (A) 49

Let AC be x. Then, by similarity ratio, $\dfrac{x}{9} = \dfrac{15}{12}$, so $x = \dfrac{45}{5}$.

126. (B) 40

Let a and b be the base lengths. Then, $\dfrac{a+b}{2} = 2r$ by the given condition. Thus, $a + b = 4r = 20$. The perimeter of $ABCD$ equals $20 + 10 + 10 = 40$.

127. (D) $10\sqrt{6}$

Let h be its height. Then, by similarity ratio, $h^2 = 24$. Thus, $h = \sqrt{24} = 2\sqrt{6}$. Therefore, the area of the triangle must be $\dfrac{1}{2} \times 2\sqrt{6} \times 10 = 10\sqrt{6}$.

128. (B) $16\sqrt{3}$

It is easy to check that $FC = 8$ and $XY = 4\sqrt{3}$. Since $XCYF$ is a rhombus, its area can be computed as $\dfrac{1}{2} \times 8 \times 4\sqrt{3} = 16\sqrt{3}$.

129. (C) 134

The perpendicular bisector of $(3, 4)$ and $(7, 1)$ passes through the center (a, r), where r is the radius of the circle. Then, $r = \dfrac{4}{3}a - \dfrac{25}{6}$. Since $a = \dfrac{6r + 25}{8}$ and $(a - 3)^2 + (r - 4)^2 = r^2$, we get $36r^2 - 500r + 1025 = 0$. The sum of the radii must be $\dfrac{500}{36} = \dfrac{125}{9}$.

130. (B) 2

First, one can apply shoelace theorem to get 2. In particular, apply it with $D(3, 6)$, $(4, 8)$, $(7, 12)$, $(6, 10)$ to get $\dfrac{1}{2}\|(24 + 48 + 70 + 36) - (24 + 56 + 72 + 30)\| = 2$.

Second, one can compute determinant on two vectors. Let $\mathbf{u} = <1, 2>$ and $\mathbf{v} = <3, 4>$. Then, the absolute value of their determinant equals 2.

131. (D) 22

It is easy to notice that the triangle ACE is equilateral. Also, let central angles from $\overline{AB} = \overline{CD} = \overline{EF}$ be α and those from $\overline{BC} = \overline{DE} = \overline{AF}$ be β. Then, $3(\alpha + \beta) = 360°$, meaning that $\alpha + \beta = 120°$. Apply the law of cosines to get $AC^2 = CE^2 = AE^2 = 4^2 + 6^2 - 2(4)(6)\cos(120°) = 76$. Since the area of ACE equals $\dfrac{\sqrt{3}}{4}AC^2$, we conclude that $19\sqrt{3}$ is its area. The answer equals $19 + 3 = 22$.

132. (B) 2

Without loss of generality, assume that $AB = 6$, $AC = 7$, and $BC = 8$. Notice that AB_AC_A is similar to ABC. Hence, r_A and r will have the length ratio between AB_AC_A and ABC. The perimeter of AB_AC_A equals 13. Similarly, the perimeter of BA_BC_B equals 14, and that of CA_CB_C equals 15. Since the perimeter of ABC equals 21, we get $r_A : r_B : r_C : r = 13 : 14 : 15 : 21$. Thus,

$$\frac{r_A + r_B + r_C}{r} = \frac{13 + 14 + 15}{21} = 2.$$

The Essential Workbook for
Competition Math
Fundamentals

초판발행 2024년 7월 30일

저자 유하림
발행인 최영민
발행처 헤르몬하우스
주소 경기도 파주시 신촌로 16
전화 031-8071-0088
팩스 031-942-8688
전자우편 hermonh@naver.com
출판등록 2015년 3월 27일
등록번호 제406-2015-31호

© 유하림 2024, Printed in Korea.

ISBN 979-11-94085-06-5 (53410)

memo

memo